# You Do You

D0588040

*Also by Sarah Knight*

## THE LIFE-CHANGING MAGIC OF
## NOT GIVING A F*CK

## GET YOUR SH*T TOGETHER

# You Do You

how to be who you are
and use what you've got
to get what you want

## Sarah Knight

Quercus

First published in Great Britain in 2017 by

Quercus Editions Ltd
Carmelite House
50 Victoria Embankment
London EC4Y 0DZ

An Hachette UK company

Copyright © Sarah Knight 2017

The moral right of Sarah Knight to be
identified as the author of this work has been
asserted in accordance with the
Copyright, Designs and Patents Act, 1988.

All rights reserved. No part of this publication
may be reproduced or transmitted in any form
or by any means, electronic or mechanical,
including photocopy, recording, or any
information storage and retrieval system,
without permission in writing from the publisher.

A CIP catalogue record for this book is available
from the British Library.

HB ISBN 978 1 78747 043 9
TPB ISBN 978 1 78747 042 2

Every effort has been made to contact copyright holders.
However, the publishers will be glad to rectify in future editions
any inadvertent omissions brought to their attention.
Quercus Editions Ltd hereby exclude all liability to the extent
permitted by law for any errors or omissions in this book and
for any loss, damage or expense (whether direct or indirect) suffered
by a third party relying on any information contained in this book.

Illustrations and hand lettering by Lauren Harms

10 9 8 7 6 5 4 3 2 1

Printed and bound in Great Britain by Clays Ltd, St Ives Plc

*Today you are You!*

*That is truer than true!*

*There is no one alive*

*who is You-er than You!*

— Dr. Seuss

# Contents

# ||

# DOs & DON'Ts: Rules for the breaking **55**

<u>|||</u>

# WILLs & WON'Ts: Not-so-great expectations    163

# IV

# You Do You

# I'm sure you're wondering why I called this meeting

Life gets exponentially better once you stop giving a fuck about what other people think and start doing what you really want to do. I know this in part because I wrote two entire books on these subjects and they've made a lot of people very happy. Perhaps you are one of those people? If so, you know that my firstborn, *The Life-Changing Magic of Not Giving a Fuck,* taught readers how to say no, set boundaries, and stop wasting time, energy, and money on things that don't bring them joy.

It was **LIBERATING.**

The sequel, *Get Your Shit Together,* taught people how to set goals and achieve them.

It was **WEAPONIZING.**

But the best part about those books — apart from two enduringly useful flowcharts that still pop up from time to time on social media — is that their success enabled me to write this one.

This one is **EMPOWERING.**

And at the risk of blowing your mind up front, the first thing I'm going to do here is unleash the most life-changing statement I've made to date. My pièce de résistance. The Mona Lisa of Dear Abbys. Your new secret weapon.

In the immortal words of Destiny's Child...are you ready for this?

# THERE

# IS

# NOTHING

WRONG
WITH
YOU.

Whoa. Are your arm hairs standing up a little straighter? Do you detect angels revving up a chorus in the next room? Perhaps you're in need of a cold shower to quell the frisson in your nethers?

Awesome. That's exactly what I was going for.

Unless...wait...maybe you just rolled your eyes and thought *This woman has obviously never spoken to my parents, bosses, coworkers, or exes, who would have told her exactly what's wrong with me. And she didn't dial up my grade school bullies, teachers, or coaches, either, because they all know a thing or two about why I lack confidence, obsess over my imperfections, and feel generally unworthy.*

Hey, now! Don't be so hard on yourself.

And okay, fiiiiiine, maybe there are a couple of things wrong with you — like you wish you were more organized, or better with money. So what? This book isn't called *You IMPROVE You.*

No, this book — *You DO You* — is about **accepting your strengths *and* your flaws,** whether those flaws are self-identified or just things that you're perfectly happy about but that other people seem to have a problem with. Or, should I say, that you WOULD be perfectly happy about, **if you felt a little more confident in yourself** and a little less worried about what other people think.*

Anyway, you seem like a good person. I have a sixth sense about these things. So, at least for the purposes of the next three hundred pages, I absolutely meant what I said a minute ago: Unless you're a serial killer or one of those people who keeps trying to start "the wave" when nobody around you is interested, **there is nothing wrong with you.**

*Then,* you may be wondering, *why did I purchase a self-help book?*

Excellent question! You're a good person *and* a quick study. I love it.

And I'll tell you why: What IS wrong — and what this nifty no-fucks-given guide shall address — is **how society burdens us with conventions, expectations, and arbitrary "norms."** And as a result, many of us struggle mightily against the **sneaky, suffocating pressure to conform** — and then spend so much time feeling bad

---

* I almost called the book *Whatever Works, Bitches!,* but I'm tired of a certain New York City–based newspaper refusing to print my titles. Don't you worry, though, my potty mouth is alive and fucking well.

about ourselves that we become convinced there *is* something wrong with us, and we flock to bookstores and seminars and gyms and weight loss cults and etiquette experts and plastic surgeons looking for the solutions to "problems" we don't even have.

You know what I'm talking about, and it's total bullshit, right?

**Well, that, my special snowflake, is precisely why I called this meeting.** Because even though there's nothing wrong with who you are, we live in a culture that right now, AT THIS VERY MOMENT, might be causing you to think otherwise.

✳  ✳  ✳

When I was growing up, I was made fun of for being too nerdy, laughing too loudly, and belting out "Hey, Buster, move!" during a junior high dance DJ's spin of the Young MC classic "Bust a Move." (For what it's worth, I had an uncle named Buster, so this did not seem weird to me, but neither did that social faux pas endear me to my peers. Kids can be *such* assholes.)

Anyway, it seemed like I could never do anything right, to fit in. The herd was traveling in one direction and I was fighting my way upstream like a buffalo with a salmon complex. To be fair, I suppose the fact that I would write that sentence proves I have an odd way of looking at the world.

But why did other kids care so damn much?

And why, as adults, should anyone keep caring whether anyone else **acts a little weird, takes a few risks, or makes some unconventional life choices** (like, say, deciding not to have any asshole kids of our own)?

The answer is: they shouldn't. But people who care about that shit aren't reading this book right now, so I'm not talking to them, I'm talking to you. I can't change them, and—pinky swear—I'm not trying to change you, either.

**What I can do is help change the way you *deal* with them and the way you *feel* about you.** (If you're into that kind of thing. No pressure.) I've been doing it for a while and it's worked out pretty well for me. In fact, *You Do You* is probably my most personal book, in terms of Tales of Challenges Overcome, though I think it's also the most universal—after all, who doesn't want to just be themselves and get through the goddamn day in whatever way works for them?

Anyone? Anyone? Bueller?

Exactly.

You needn't have been mocked at a sixth-grade dance to understand the sting of judgment or feel the pressure to conform. That can happen at any age and under many circumstances — like when you move to a new city, start a new job, or marry into a new clan. Maybe you're a born contrarian. Maybe you're a savant. Maybe you mixed plaids with stripes one day and decided you liked it. Lord have mercy!

Whatever the case, if you came to this book **feeling different, misunderstood, frustrated, or constrained by** your parents, siblings, neighbors, roommates, bosses, coworkers, Tinder matches, significant others, or society-at-large — well, I'm sorry to hear that, but you're in the right place.

And this may sound like a tall order, but in addition to helping you accept who you are, I'm going to help you find confidence in your beliefs, your attitude, your looks, your goals, and your all-around swagger. Because all of the qualities — yes, even the flaws — that make you, YOU, also make you **interesting, capable, and powerful** in your own way.

You just need to own them.

## What "you doing you" looks like

The advice in this book boils down to one simple mantra: **Stand up for who you are and what you want.** How do you do that? **Stop letting other people tell you what to do, how to do it, or why it can't be done.**\*

Each part of *You Do You* builds the argument for **living life on your own terms**. It covers:

- The Tyranny of "Just Because"
- Lowest Common Denominator Living, and why you deserve better
- WNDs (what you want, need, and deserve)
- The social contract, what it's for, and where it fails
- Doubters, haters, and other judgy motherfuckers
- Turning your flaws into strengths — aka "mental redecorating"
- When it's okay to be selfish, why it's pointless to be perfect, how to be "difficult," and much, much more!

---

\* Yes, this is an ironic sentiment from someone who makes her living telling other people what to do, but I didn't become a bestselling anti-guru by following the rules, now did I?

## Part I ("YOU ARE HERE: An orientation exercise")

In this section, I'll walk you through the "social contract"—a collection of unspoken yet extremely potent rules, expectations, and obligations that may not be serving you as well as they could. Then I'll give you a sneak peek at fifteen of its most nefarious clauses, my amendments to which will shape the rest of the book. Gimmicky? Yes. A snazzy way to organize my thoughts and marshal my arguments? That too.

## Part II ("DOs & DON'Ts: Rules for the breaking")

Here we'll focus on the kinds of rules you learned in kindergarten that don't necessarily apply to life as an adult, such as "Don't be selfish" and "Do be a team player." I'll show you how to bend or break a few of these with an eye toward improving your life and—just as important—not ruining anybody else's along the way.

## Part III ("WILLs & WON'Ts: Not-so-great expectations")

This is where you'll learn how to ignore or straight-up defy people who have the nerve to tell you what will happen or how you'll feel as a result of *your* life choices. In the chapter called "You will regret that" I'll talk about making decisions that seem wrong to others but feel oh-so-right to you, and in "You won't get anywhere with that attitude," I'll extoll the power of pessimism in helping you plan ahead and avoid disappointment—aka managing your *own* expectations.

## Part IV ("SHOULDs & SHOULDN'Ts: Much too much obliged")

If you've had it up to HERE with fulfilling random, stupid obligations set forth by society—whether to be nice or thin or to act submissive or sane—then Part IV is exactly what the doctor respectfully suggested. In "You should smile more," I'll explain why it's not your job to be nice, and in "You shouldn't act so crazy," I'll reminisce about the time I snuck a litter box and ten buckets of craft sand into my office and hoped nobody would notice. Today? I'd put that shit on Instagram Stories. Because I finally understand that I'm not obligated to speak or act in any way that robs me of living an authentic life.

And neither are you.

✳ ✳ ✳

I wrote *You Do You* for people like me, who just want to do their own thing and stop caring about how their desires, motivations, opinions, and decisions are being questioned, dissected, and judged by others. **For misfits, rebels, black sheep, and unicorns.** For folks who want to wear white after Labor Day or spread pimento cheese on their Pop-Tarts; for those who prefer to stay single in a culture that fetishizes elaborate engagement videos or who drop out of med school to open a medical marijuana dispensary.

Shine on, you crazy diamonds.

I wrote it for **all of us who feel pressured to follow rules, meet expectations, and fulfill obligations** — and who don't like it one bit. I wrote it for kids, college students, parents, and retirees, and for grandmas who left their husbands of four decades to spend their golden years with a "friend" named Mary. I wrote it for readers of my previous books but also for people who've never even heard of "that foul-mouthed anti-guru Sarah Knight."

And finally, I wrote it because **being yourself *should* be the easiest thing in the world**: Wake up, confirm no *Freaky Friday* shit has occurred, and go about your day. Yet so many of us struggle with that — as children, as adults, as lesbian grandmas. We've convinced ourselves (or let other people convince us) that there's something wrong with us. We lack confidence in our individuality and we feel compelled to conform — to be like everyone else, "fix" our "flaws," and toe the boring ol' cultural party line.

But what if there isn't anything wrong with us? **What if there really, truly, isn't anything wrong with YOU?**

That's the premise I'm working from, and I think it's mighty goddamn refreshing.

So instead of trying to change you, let's celebrate what it means to *be* you — in all your weird, difficult, selfish, imperfect, antisocial, overexcited, unique, and unconventional ways. Let's harness those "flaws" and turn them into strengths. And let's set the record straight for all the doubters and haters who sent you running for a self-help book in the first place.

I mean, I appreciate the business, but fuck those people. Come on, let's do you!

# 1

# YOU ARE HERE:
## An orientation exercise

I tested my parents' urge to smother me with my own blankie in many ways as a small child, including by refusing to take no for an answer. I mean, I was like a dog with a motherfucking *bone*. As their patience wore thin, and after they'd exhausted other options, Mom and Dad would inevitably start answering, "Just because."

As in:

"Can we pleeeeeeease go to Funtown today?"

"No."

"Why not?"

"Because it's too late."

"Okay, so can we go tomorrow?"

"No."

"Why not?"

"Because it will be closed."

"So can we go the day after that?"

"No."

"How come?"

"JUST...BECAUSE!"

To which I would reply, "But *why* because?"

Yes, I was a giant pain in the ass, but it turns out I was onto something. I had happened upon—and refused to back down in the face of—the **Tyranny of "Just Because."**

I've continued to ask "Why because?" throughout my life, and not only when I'm denied access to cotton candy and Ferris wheels. For example: the words "social butterfly," "optimist," and "mama bear" do not describe me, so why would I go to the party of the year *just because* I got invited? Why should I look on the bright side *just because* someone told me to? And what if I have no intention of starting a family *just because* that's what all my friends are doing these days?

Oh, the tyranny!

**The biggest obstacle to doing you is doing things *just* because that's how everyone else does them, or because it's the way those things have always been done.** And when you deny your true nature *just because* you're trying to fit in with the crowd — then you're not doing you, **YOU'RE SCREWING YOU.**

Why would you want to do that?

Why because?

*You Do You* addresses the Tyranny of "Just Because" (for all kinds of people, not just the antisocial, pessimistic, child-free ones like me) and offers inspiration, advice, and talking points for the next time you feel the need to justify your life choices — whether to yourself, to your parents, or to a waiter who thinks a well-done burger is "an insult to the beef."

(You do you, guy. But if it comes out medium rare, you may find your tip somewhat insulting too.)

Coming up in Part I, we'll rap about **who you are and why you're reading this book;** I'll ask you some questions about **what you want, need, and deserve from life;** and I'll describe a malady that is not yet in the *DSM* but certainly should be, and to which *You Do You* offers the cure.

Then we'll examine the social contract and I'll describe when you should adhere to it — before showing exactly when, why, and how you should not. Part of that "how" involves **mental redecorating,** which is a companion to the mental decluttering my other books are known for. This is the simple, painless process by which we'll be turning your flaws (or what other people *allege* to be your flaws) into strengths — so that you may ignore the doubters, silence the haters, and do you with the exuberance of Bill Clinton at a balloon party. On Ecstasy. With interns.

Finally, we'll go over **what it means to be "unconventional"** and why that is a messy, meaningless label but nevertheless germane to every page of this book.

Oh, and one more thing. I am nothing if not consistent — and mindful of how a kicky flowchart helps build my brand — so here's a visual teaser for everything

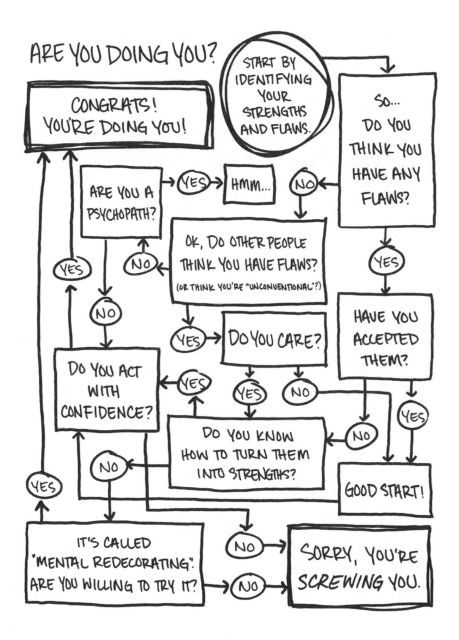

Part I has to offer. (This is just supplemental material, not an excuse to skip ahead. Don't get cocky.)

# Just who do you think you are?

**Let's start with the bad news:** I don't have the answer to the above question. I can listen to your problems, I can accept you for you, and I can nod in solidarity or pat you on the back in sympathy. But I can't tell you who you are. Only you can do that. (Or, like, maybe astrologers can do that? I don't know. Like I said, not my department.)

**Now for the good news:** In my humble, unscientific opinion, most people already know who they are and what makes them happy. They may not know exactly how to be that person or get that life, but that's what I'm here for. And if you don't know off the top of your head who you are and what you want, I bet that if given the opportunity and absolutely zero outside pressure, you could figure it out.

(Did I mention I'm going to need you to do that before we can move forward?)

**Don't worry, though, figuring yourself out is not as intimidating as it sounds.** Playing "Who do you think you are?" is like playing a video game, and even a seven-year-old with ADD can do that.

## Ready player one

The first thing you do in lots of video games is choose a character. Let's use Nintendo's go-kart racing classic *Mario Kart* as an example. (You don't have to know anything about *Mario Kart* to follow along here, but if you have played it and gotten the top score on the "Bowser's Castle" level, hearty congrats.)

In Mario World, you could be Princess Peach, who rides fast but spins out easily when hit, or a slow, methodical koopa named Bowser, who doesn't get rattled when other players get up in your grill. (Koopas are anthropomorphic turtles. Again, not my department.) Or you could be one of two unflappable Italian brothers who run a successful plumbing business by day and chill out at the track on weekends. Mario and Luigi are just here to enjoy the ride.

**You pick your character based on their strengths (and in exchange, you accept their weaknesses). Which one suits your style of play and creates the best outcome for you?**

I myself have pitiable reflexes, so I prefer a slower, heavier kart that's less likely to go over the edge after a crash. You may have more dexterous thumbs and be willing to risk a lightweight chassis for the benefits of reliably leaving Bowser in your dust. Maybe the power of invisibility is preferable to the power of hurling fireballs at your competitors. You do you.

And since right now it's just you, me, and a bag of Doritos, how about you also take this *conveniently provided* opportunity to identify some strengths and weaknesses that are more pertinent to your daily life.

Are you loud? Quiet? Big? Small? Quirky? Selfish, difficult, negative, or weird? And which column do those belong in, anyway?

Jot down a few of them here — no need for an exhaustive catalog, just a little something to get the juices flowing:

| MY STRENGTHS | MY WEAKNESSES |
| --- | --- |
| _____ | _____ |
| _____ | _____ |
| _____ | _____ |
| _____ | _____ |

Next step in the game: choosing a "world" to play in. In *Mario Kart,* it would be a racetrack, such as Ghost Valley, Mushroom Gorge, or Moo Moo Meadows, among many others. Each has its pros and cons, but you would pick one to play based on how much fun it is for YOU.

This is a metric that shouldn't be too hard to define, right?

Well, in life, you can also choose among various tracks: family man in the 'burbs, world traveler on the global stage, philanthropist, elite athlete, hot-dog-eating-contest champion. You can even play more than one at a time, because metaphors are not infallible and life is more complex than a video game. Regardless, only you can know which one(s) make you happy.

**What's your ideal world?**

Try to come up with a sentence or two that describes it. There won't be a quiz or anything, but writing this shit down is useful. Trust me.

_____

_____

_____

All set? Great, now let's talk about what happens when
you exit the two-dimensional confines of Mario World:

- When you're faced with real-life decisions that impact
  your real-life happiness, do you plot your own course,
  design your own character, and play to your strengths?
  Or do you go with the computer-assigned role?

- Do you feel comfortable, safe, and confident in
  your choices? Or are you just hoping to squeak by
  in the middle of the pack without getting run off
  the road by an anthropomorphic turtle?

These are the tough questions, and yes, I lulled you
into submission and then snuck them in. But you don't
have to write down your answers, because we already
both know them. If you _were_ playing to your strengths
and you _did_ feel comfortable, safe, and confident in your
choices, then you'd be out there kicking koopa ass and

taking koopa names instead of reading this book and sucking nacho cheese dust off your fingers.

Hey, man, don't hate the player. Hate the game.

No, if you're still with me by now, I'm guessing your problem isn't who you are or what makes you happy; **your problem is that you feel like it's not *okay* to be that person and want those things.**

And why do you feel that way? Well, probably because other people are always telling you you're too loud, too quiet, too big, too small, too crazy, too quirky, too selfish, too difficult, too negative, and "Hey, while we're at it, STOP BEING SO WEIRD, *WEIRDO*."

Yep. Been there, heard that.

If you hear it enough, life starts to feel like an infinite go-kart circuit where the most prudent path lies in riding the slipstream of the player in front of you — a disorder that is known (by me) as **Lowest Common Denominator Living**.


## Lowest Common Denominator Living

This condition is evinced by the urge to stifle any or all unconventional, unusual, uncommon, odd, novel, rebellious, or unpopular aspects of one's personality, lifestyle, or value system — **and results in "just getting by" as opposed to "getting on with your bad self."**

If LCD Living describes your current circumstances, tell me, why should you waste another day in its clammy, limp handshake of a grip?

Especially when I can *personally guarantee* that it's fun (and productive) to speak your mind in a meeting without caring whether people think you're being difficult; it's satisfying to tell your boss the truth instead of drinking the tainted Kool-Aid of office diplomacy; it's an incredible relief to confess to a roomful of Southern ladies that you have absolutely no opinion whatsoever about china patterns; and it's healthy to let it all hang out wherever, whenever a Shaggy song comes over the airwaves.*

**Now for the best news of all:** No matter what form your you-ness takes — princess, plumber, koopa — it makes no difference to me. Nor does it affect your ability to benefit from my advice. *You Do You* crosses sex, gender, age, cultural, and socioeconomic lines, **because I'm helping you from the inside out, not the outside in.**

---

* Yeah, that's right. It WAS me.

### A few caveats

If you are the guy who worked in my khaki-scented corporate office and dressed like a member of the Village People every single day, you need no help from me in the "express yourself" department. You, sir, are an inspiration to us all.

If you're the person who tweeted: "Started asking the folks at Chipotle to individually package my ingredients so I can assemble it all at home" accompanied by a photo of seven two-ounce containers of toppings, then you can bow out of the "How to be 'difficult'" seminar on page 109.

And if you are my husband, who has been known to meow the entirety of "We Are the World" *in the timbre of each individual singer,* you are basically the Brand Ambassador for Weird and may therefore skip the section on "letting your freak flag fly." (Ooh, but maybe you should make a guest appearance on the audiobook. I'll have my people call your people.)

Now, in order to keep you safe from the scourge of Lowest Common Denominator Living, we're going to have to **reestablish your relationship to yourself and to the rest of the world.**

Again, this is not as hard as it sounds.

In a few pages, I'll take you through the social contract

and begin the amendment process, which continues through the rest of the book. But the social contract is just that — "social" — and therefore all tied up in your relationship to others. Before we can unpack that crate of cabbage, we need to talk about your relationship to *yourself.*

I've decided to talk about it using acronyms and Jesus. Hey, I do me.

# WNDs and the second half of the Golden Rule

You may have heard of something called the Golden Rule: **Do unto others as you would have them do unto you.** This twenty-four-carat nugget is paraphrased from the Bible, but regardless of its origin, it seems both reasonable and feasible, does it not?

(You might even say it underlies the entire social contract, and you would not be wrong. Hang tight.)

But it also seems clear — even to someone like me who last attended Sunday Mass when Wham! had two of the top three songs of the year—that you can't *follow* the Golden Rule if you don't first establish HOW YOU WOULD LIKE PEOPLE TO DO UNTO YOU.

In other words: **What do you *want*, *need*, and *deserve* from life?**

These are your **WNDs**. Not to be confused with WMDs, WNDs do not endanger the lives of innocent villagers or provide governments with an excuse to engage in an eight-year, multitrillion-dollar war. But just like WMDs, if you can't identify them…you've got a big problem.

So, earlier in the book you spent some time figuring out who you are and what you're playing for. Now, what do you want, need, and deserve in order to get there?

I'll go first, to give you an example:

I **want** to make my own decisions.

I **need** to take care of my mental health.

I **deserve** to have my opinions heard.

If you intend to get the most out of *You Do You*, you're going to have to answer those questions too. What makes you happy? What tickles your pickle?

I **want** _____.

I **need** _____.

I **deserve** _____.

(By the way, your WNDs need not be limited to the available surface of this relatively small page. Feel free to get yourself a notebook, start dictating into your iPhone, or graffiti a wall if you have to. The important thing is to identify them and keep a close watch over them as life goes on. It's for your own good, not just the innocent villagers'.)

Once you've clarified your half of the Golden Rule and shored up those WNDs, we can achieve all kinds of pickle-ticklin' goodness by negotiating — with the rest of the world — the best terms the social contract has to offer.

For YOU.

# The social contract

The minute we exit the birth canal, we enter into **a set of guidelines for human behavior that we all agree to follow (more or less) so we can live our lives in peace.**

What's known as the "social contract" is not a legal document, or even a tangible one, but just because its clauses haven't been typed out and stored in a fireproof safe-deposit box with all of our important paperwork doesn't mean we don't know it's there.

And boy, does it come in handy sometimes.

We all have to share space in the world — on highways, in dorm rooms, and in the pit at a Jamiroquai concert — and sometimes, shit happens that tests our capacity for reason and restraint. During those times, **the social contract acts as a buffer to our baser instincts.** It steers us back from the brink of road rage; keeps us off the dean's shit list; and stops us at the last possible second from using a lighter to set fire to the hair of the girl who muscled her way in front of us even though we had been at the venue for HOURS before she and her oblivious friend showed up with their stupid fucking backpacks. (What? I said it stopped me.)

And I *completely* agree that there are clauses we should all observe: such as "Do not whip out your cell phone in the middle of a Broadway musical," "Do not answer the door nude when folks come a-caroling," and "Do not post unflattering photos of your friends on social media."

But there are other clauses — lots of 'em — that we shouldn't adhere to "just because." Some have the potential to hurt us more than they help others; some are out of date, out of vogue, or out of touch; and some threaten to upset the very balance that the social contract was put in place to maintain.

These are the ones that lead, directly or indirectly, to a nasty case of LCD Living.

I chose fifteen of my least favorite to focus on — such as **"Don't be selfish"** and **"You will regret that"** — and I've amended them to suit a much wider swathe of humanity, including but not limited to: weirdos, pessimists, loners, hot messes, and people who definitely will not regret that, but thanks for your concern.

Here's a sneak peek at what's on tap in Parts II to IV:

# THE SOCIAL CONTRACT *

## *WITH AMENDMENTS

1) **Don't be selfish***

   * It is absolutely okay—and healthy—to be concerned with your own self-interest, which you can do while *also* looking out for others. Being selfish and being selfless don't have to be mutually exclusive.

2) **Do your best***

   * Ambition and integrity are great qualities, but it's hard to accomplish anything when both hands are occupied by scratching your stress-induced hives.

3) **Don't be difficult***

   * Stand up for yourself—and for other people. Having the courage of your convictions isn't being "difficult." It's admirable, and it will also get you a better table.

4) **Do be a team player***

   * Go your own way, if that's what sizzles your bacon. Who fucking cares how you do it, as long as it gets done? (Or doesn't get done. See amendment to clause 2, above.)

5) **Don't quit your day job** *

   * Develop a healthy attitude toward risk and don't let the doubters and haters stop you from taking one when the time is right. Also: fear is just another word for suffocating your dreams with a big blue tarp.

6) **You will change your mind** *

   * Maybe, but if you do, no biggie. Don't let other people's opinions about *your* life choices — especially the "unconventional" ones — keep you from being true to yourself.

7) **You won't get anywhere with that attitude** *

   * Whatever fuels you, whatever keeps you feeling safe, and whatever helps you sleep tonight and enjoy your vacation tomorrow is the right attitude for you.

8) **You will regret that** *

   * If at first people don't succeed in changing your mind, they will try, try again by filling your head with tales of potential woe. Don't listen to them.

9) **You won't get a good job if you don't go to college** *

   * Success is yours to define. Nobody needs a diploma — literal or metaphorical — to tell them what feels good.

10) **You will never live that down** *

   * If you're freaky and you know it, clap your hands. And if not, some polite applause for the rest of us wouldn't hurt.

11) **You should always put family first** *

   * Please feel free to value all of the wonderful people in your life equally. There, was that so hard?

12) **You shouldn't act so crazy** *

   * Mental health is just as important as physical health, and if tending to yours means being open about its care and feeding, go nuts.

13) **You should smile more** *

   * Kindly fuck off.

14) **You shouldn't eat that** *

   * Accept your body for what it is rather than punishing it for what it isn't. And save me some pizza.

15) **You should check your ego at the door** *

   * If you don't have confidence in yourself, who will? Own it, talk with it, walk with it, and don't forget to congratulate yourself on a daily basis. You've earned it.

The trick is to implement all of these amendments and "do you" without ripping up the social contract altogether, pissing on it, and burning it in an empty oil drum on your neighbor's lawn. That's not going to get you anywhere — except, perhaps, hauled in front of a very stern judge.

Lucky for you, this isn't my first rodeo. Not even my second, actually.

In *The Life-Changing Magic of Not Giving a Fuck,* I showed readers **how to stop giving a fuck without turning into an asshole** — by way of the NotSorry Method, which is based in honesty and politeness. The same principle applies here. The idea is to live your life with more happiness and harmony, not to make enemies in the name of doing you.

In *Get Your Shit Together,* I explained **"how to win at life without being an insufferable prick."** Basically, having a great life isn't about trash-talking, competing with, or elbowing other people out of your way. It's about identifying your *own* goals and going after them. The goal of this book — living an authentic life — may be somewhat more nebulous, but the rules of the game are the same. Eyes on your own paper.

So I still say: **Don't be an asshole or an insufferable prick.** Words to live by. But with regard to doing you, I have one further caution:

**Don't be a psychopath.**

*You Do You* is emphatically NOT a manual for leaving decency, personal responsibility, and empathy by the wayside, and I did emphatically NOT spend so many increasingly frantic months writing it so that anyone could use it as an excuse for such chicanery.

**You can amend the social contract to give yourself a break** *while* **remaining a fundamentally good person.** (BONUS: You'll probably wind up a happier person too.)

But if you're having a hard time reconciling this stuff, please refer to the following helpful guidelines for not being a psychopath:

---

### Helpful guidelines for not being a psychopath

1. Feel good about yourself, not good about fucking with other people just for the fun of it.
2. Don't equate "doing you" with "being irresponsible."
3. Recognize when doing you has consequences, and accept them.
4. Have empathy for everyone else who's out there trying to do them.
5. Be comfortable in your own skin, not comfortable making a suit out of someone else's.

---

## Before you sign on the dotted line

In any agreement, there are limits to the rights you should be expected to give up — and within the social contract, the right to be yourself is A-NUMBER-ONE. Next on that list: the right to act with confidence and conviction; the right to be a little selfish, imperfect, or difficult when you feel like it; and the right to spice it up with jazz hands every once in a while.

So before you trot out the old John Hancock, the pertinent questions are:

**What do I owe myself?**

**What do I owe others?**

**And how can I negotiate the best deal for the former without totally fucking over the latter?**

# Meet Judgy McJudgerson

After the Tyranny of "Just Because," the next biggest obstacle to you doing you — and one that I will spend a *massive* amount of time railing against in the next couple hundred pages — is **other people who don't understand it or just plain don't like it.**

These are **the doubters and the haters,** whom I shall refer to unilaterally by the moniker "Judgy McJudgerson."

# A TAXONOMY OF JUDGYS

| DOUBTERS | HATERS |
|---|---|
| People who don't get your style | People who are jealous of your style |
| People who think you're going to fail | People who want you to fail |
| People who aren't sure you should be doing that | People who think whatever you're doing is stupid |
| People who write off your ideas | People who shit on your ideas |
| People who think they know what's best for you | People who don't care what's best for you |

Back in virtual Mario World, I had you identify some of your weaknesses. (In case you haven't figured it out yet, you really do need to go back and write those down; they're going to become important in about three pages.) As we go on, you'll get more and more comfortable working around them, using your strengths as ballast. But the Judgy McJudgersons of the world exist to throw you off course, and to combat Judgy's bad juju, you're going to need a little help.

Enter: mental redecorating.

# Mental redecorating

If you've read my other books, you know I invented **"mental decluttering,"** which, like physical decluttering, has two steps:

1. Discarding (e.g., giving fewer fucks)

2. Organizing (e.g., getting your shit together)

If you haven't read those books, well, that's the gist. Mental decluttering helps you inventory your life, decide what brings you joy and what annoys the ever-loving crap out of you, and retain the former and kick the latter to the curb.

At the heart of *You Do You*, however, is something different. Sort of **fêng shui with a side of "fuck that shit,"** mental *redecorating* is low on time commitment and extremely high on improving your current circumstances.

I'm not talking a full-scale remodel—there are other gurus for that, if you're into Pilates and masochism.*

Sometimes all a room needs is a new coat of paint, a dimmer switch—or maybe you move that chair over by the window and put the TV on the mantel. There, doesn't that flow better?

Well, just like real-world redecorating refreshes an existing space, mental redecorating refreshes your outlook on life. **It helps you emphasize (or de-emphasize) what's already there** instead of making fundamental changes that are either impossible or, frankly, unwarranted. And as with its ancient Chinese cousin, *fêng shui,* mental redecorating takes things that are getting in the way and reorients them so they work WITH you, not against you.

It has two steps, because two-step methods is just how I roll:

### 1. Identify your weaknesses
You—or Judgy—might call those weaknesses your "flaws," but I just call them "what makes you, you."

---

* And you can do it without having read either of my other books, though obviously I'm high on the whole kit and caboodle.

## 2. Refresh the way you look at or deal with them (or both!)

Remember, there is nothing wrong with you. Just because Judgy sees something as an eyesore — like an old wingback chair with worn armrests — doesn't mean you can't show it off proudly. It's shabby chic! Anthropologie makes a lot of money off that shit.

**Recasting your weaknesses as strengths could be just the thing you need to become [mentally] house-proud:**

## TURNING YOUR WEAKNESSES INTO STRENGTHS

| WEAKNESS | ➜ REDECORATE IT! ➜ | STRENGTH |
|---|---|---|
| NERDY | It's not just a stamp collection, it's an investment in your future. | SMART |

| WEAKNESS → | REDECORATE IT! → | STRENGTH |
|---|---|---|
| STUBBORN | A cast-iron gnome is annoying to mow around, but it won't blow away in a storm. | PERSEVER-ANT |
| PESSIMISTIC | Hoarding one too many Allen wrenches in the junk drawer? You'll be ready when the bed collapses. | REALISTIC |
| WEIRD | That bathtub in the living room is no accident — it's called a "statement piece." | UNIQUE |

I do this myself when Judgy calls me "difficult." He thinks he should be able to walk all over me like I'm some cheap frat house rug, but he is mistaken, for I am a fine Moroccan tapestry that was worth sourcing, transporting on someone's lap for the ten-hour flight home, and hanging on the wall, far away from dumb muddy boat shoes.

Judgy also claims that selfishness, like orange paisley wallpaper, is no way to create a space where everyone enjoys hanging out. But I'm here to tell you that a judiciously applied accent wall can make you happy, *without* giving your guests any seizures. (More on that in "Don't be selfish" on page 62.)

**Yes, a focused bout of mental redecorating can stimulate self-acceptance, boost confidence, and hone your ability to ignore the doubters and shut down the haters from here on out.**

For shits and giggles, let's try it on those weaknesses you listed back on page 27, when you were suiting up for a pleasure cruise through Moo Moo Meadows. (Or the ones you went back and filled in a minute ago because I shamed you.) I promise, soon mental redecorating will be second nature and you won't have to hunch over a little book recording your notes like you're Jane Fucking Goodall observing chimpanzees in Tanzania — but for now, just humor me, will ya?

## TURNING YOUR WEAKNESSES
## INTO STRENGTHS

WEAKNESS ➔ REDECORATE IT! ➔ STRENGTH

_____

_____    _____    _____

_____    _____    _____

_____    _____    _____

_____

# Unconventional wisdom for unconventional people

At this point I'd like to congratulate you on both your initial gumption and your attention span. Marvelous, truly! You're on your way to doing you with the best of them. But before we move into Part II, I want to clarify one more thing: You're going to see me trot out the word "unconventional" quite a bit, so we need to talk about what that means, at least within these pages.

In order to get some background on potential readers

of *You Do You,* I conducted an anonymous survey that I'll refer to throughout the book (possibly more than my editor would like me to, given its highly unscientific nature). In it, I asked if the respondent would consider themselves unconventional — or if other people would — and if so, why.

**These were some of the answers:**

I'm not as tied to traditions as other people are.

I do what I want, I wear what I want, I say what I (really) think.

I've got purple hair and tattoos.

I'm gay.

I'm bisexual.

I'm not very feminine.

I prefer to be alone.

I don't want children and am not close to my family.

I'm utterly disinterested in following the default procedure.

I have quirky fashion sense.

I moved abroad at 21, which none of my school friends did.

I'm happily single.

I was homeschooled.

I'm really strong in my faith.

I'm an atheist.

I'm just kind of weird (in a good way) and have really niche interests.

I don't mind sharing embarrassing details about my life.

I'm a redheaded, left-handed woman who swears, drinks, and laughs loudly.

I just do my own thing.

Ugh, this question.

So when I talk about "being unconventional," this is the kind of stuff I mean. Mind you, I'm not saying I think it's abnormal or weird to want to live alone or get tattooed or buck tradition — just that these are the types of barriers put up by convention, which caters to history, tradition, lack of options, lack of imagination, and/or the Tyranny of "Just Because."

We have to figure out our own way around these barriers if we want to (a) be happy and (b) have fewer reasons to fill out anonymous online surveys using the word "Ugh."

For my part, I'm going to offer a bunch of *unconventional* wisdom to help people like you (and me) survive in a conventional world.

Such as: **"You might die tomorrow, so be selfish today"**; **"Pretend you're a toddler"**; and **"When in doubt, dance a jig."**

# Leaning in to being you

It's your life. Living it authentically means working with what you've got, and making the best of it.

Want to dye your hair purple, quit your job and start a trout hatchery, or refuse to wear long pants even when it's reeeeeally cold out? **You do you.**

Fancy yourself a lone wolf, eschewing marriage and kids for a life of tranquil solitude and nobody else's pee on the seat? **You do you.**

Want to raise hell when something is important to you, act crazy when you feel like it, and see the glass as half empty if negativity is what motivates you to get shit done? **YOU. DO. YOU.**

By the end of the book, I hope you'll feel more accepting of and confident in being yourself. And I *know* you'll be armed with plenty of ammunition to lean in hard the next time anyone makes you feel — explicitly or implicitly — like there's something wrong with you.

Once more, for the people in the back:

# THERE ISN'T.

Now let's amend that social contract, shall we? I think you'll find my new clauses to your liking.

# 11

# DOs & DON'Ts:
# Rules for the breaking

Rules come in all shapes and sizes. Spoken rules, unspoken rules, passive-aggressive signage at the public pool. They're usually there for a reason, but many of them are not as indisputable as you've been led to believe.

For example, "Always flush after number two" is a solid entry in the social contract. (Seriously, who raised you?) Whereas "Be nice to your elders" is a good suggestion in theory, but plenty of elders can be real dirtbags. Have you met Clint Eastwood? I think it's okay to interpret that one on a case-by-case basis.

For most of my life, I was big on following ALL OF THE RULES; spoken, unspoken, indisputable, or otherwise. In some ways, this worked out well for me. Like, I've never had to have my best friend call my parents while I sobered up in the back of a squad car. Then again, my brother seems to have had a bit more fun in his twenties than I did.

Conclusion: rules that are also "laws" are probably best left unchallenged.

But in the past few years, I started noticing that other rules — some of the unspoken, non-legally-enforceable ones — were **holding me back more than they were helping me.** And that my following them wasn't really helping anybody *else*, either. So I broke a few. And what do you know? I've actually achieved more happiness and success since I stopped being such a stickler for "doing stuff the way most people think it should be done."

It started with little things, like skipping the weekly marketing meeting at my last job. (Readers of *The Life-Changing Magic of Not Giving a Fuck* will recall that meetings are a frequent casualty of one's slimmed-down Fuck Budget.)

After a few years of getting up an extra hour early on Thursdays just to sit in a room while people recited updates that were unrelated to *me* getting *my* work done, I decided enough was enough. If one of my projects was on the agenda (once every five or six weeks), of course I'd make the effort. Otherwise, I'd spend that hour catching forty additional glorious winks.

I'd be doing unto others exactly like I'd want them to do unto me, i.e., "not getting up an extra hour early for the privilege of packing into a too-small conference room together to watch my lips move *just because* everyone else is doing it." My absence wouldn't be hurting anyone, I reasoned, and I certainly wouldn't miss the low-level fug of coffee breath, passive-aggressive pissing matches among my colleagues, or the occasional tray of picked-over bagels.

Furthermore, who would really miss *me*?

As it turned out, nobody except one stickler-for-the-rules coworker who pestered me every Thursday when he spied me rolling into the office at my usual 10 a.m. Okay, 10:15.

(O-KAYYYY, 10:30. Jeez, you drive a hard bargain.)

"Where were you?" this fellow would ask. "Do you think this meeting is *optional*?" He was joking. Sort of. He knew the marketing meeting wasn't mandatory for non-marketing staff, but he really felt like we (the editorial staff) *should* be there, and that if he had to follow the rules, so should I.

To be fair, I'd thought that too, for three wildly misinformed years. But when I decided to **break an unspoken rule of office etiquette** ("If you have to suffer through this mind-numbing bullshit, so should everyone else"), my life got tangibly better. By my back-of-the-envelope calculations, I saved myself at least forty hours — or one full-time workweek — of precious, blessed sleep each subsequent year.

Can't beat that with a stale sesame seed bagel.

This, ladies and gentlemen, is a USDA prime example

of when it's okay to break a rule. Not only did it benefit me without hurting anyone else, it opened up an extra 2.2 cubic feet of space for another poor soul who *did* have to be there, and it surely emboldened others who didn't.

I'm a role model, is what I'm saying.

With this success in my back pocket, my rule-breaking began to take more audacious forms. I flouted dress codes and wore flip-flops every day, not just Friday. I decided to get loud about my opinions instead of sitting idly by and avoiding confrontation. Occasionally, I brought only my B+ game.

It felt good.

**"Rules are rules!" you might say. But now *I* say, "Eh, most of them are just suggestions."**

Along with reducing my day-to-day stress and making me feel more confident and empowered, breaking some of these unwritten rules made me a better employee, and a better person in general. It's a lot easier to be creative and industrious when you're focused on real challenges rather than "suggested" ones. And when you go out with your friends or home to your partner after a calm, productive day, you're a lot more fun to be *around* too.

## Starting some Dumpster fires

Another rule I like to break is one you may not even know about. And if you don't know about it, you might think it's weird that the word "Dumpster" is capitalized here and in the heading above. I think it's weird too. But because I've spent some time around copyeditors, I happen to know that the word "Dumpster" is a legally protected trademark and therefore should always be capitalized, even though most people use it generically to refer to a big trash container, not necessarily a Dumpster-branded one. (The same goes for "Kleenex," which you probably use interchangeably with "tissue," as you do "Jeep" for "any old sport utility vehicle.") That said, in my nonprofessional life — i.e., on social media — I've started to rebel! Thanks to one Donald J. Trump, I've had endless opportunities to use the term "dumpster fire" on Twitter, and I refuse to capitalize it. My way may not be technically correct, but it looks better, and if anyone should get sued over careless statements on their Twitter feed, I think a certain world leader is way ahead of me in the queue.

The key to doing you (without becoming a psychopath) is knowing which rules are bend- and breakable, and how to do it in a constructive way. One "rule" of thumb is: **If it's hurting or limiting you *more* than it's helping others, it's a good candidate.**

To help get you started on identifying and thwarting such, I'll be highlighting **five dos and don'ts from the social contract — like I said, my least favorites —** and offering an alternate perspective on each. Where "alternate perspective" means "a completely opposite point of view that some people will never accept but that makes a lot of damn sense if you just give it a second to sink in."

For example, in **"Don't Be Selfish"** I'll explain why selflessness is overrated and how looking out for number one is often in everybody's best interests, not just your own. In **"Do Your Best,"** I'll write a letter to my younger self that functions as a cautionary tale for perfectionists of all ages. I'll also cover standing up for what you believe in (**"Don't Be Difficult"**), striking out on your own (**"Do Be a Team Player"**), and taking calculated risks (**"Don't Quit Your Day Job"**).

By the time you're done doing the don'ts and don'ting the dos, we'll be ready to tackle a more insidious cause of Lowest Common Denominator Living known as "other people's expectations."

But that's in Part III. For now, whatever you do, don't turn the page.

# Don't Be Selfish\*

*\*Life is short. Reclaim the word.*

In the last few years, I've made it my mission to **destigmatize selfishness.** I know, lofty goal, but somebody has to do it.

In *The Life-Changing Magic of Not Giving a Fuck,* I wrote about being selfish in terms of getting rid of stuff you don't want — not just objects, but also obligations, relationships, events, and anything in life that annoys you. Why spend time you don't have with people you don't like, doing things you don't want to do? You can make a big dent in all that crap with mental decluttering — **selfishly setting boundaries and saying no so that you can focus instead on what brings you joy.**

*Get Your Shit Together* included a whole section on **the selfish pursuit of "me time,"** which I suggested scheduling the same way you would any necessary appointment — because if you don't set aside time for a bubble bath or a round of golf, who will? Your boss is busy assigning you tasks, your friends are busy sending you Evites, and your kid is busy refusing to take the very naps that you would murder a hobo for right now. You need that me time to recharge your batteries so you can DO all those tasks, ENJOY all those parties, and NOT MURDER YOUR CHILDREN OR ANY HOBOS.

So here in *You Do You,* I'm tripling down.

I shall begin my all-out assault on the social contract with the rule that informs all the other rules, and one that, I'm certain, you've been *expressly taught* not to break. Why? Because as far as I'm concerned, **selfishness is a perfectly healthy quality,** and under the right circumstances (hint: lots of them), "Be selfish!" is even better advice.

If you've been a good boy or girl your whole life, embracing this idea might feel not only weird, but *wrong.* I hear ya. Like, literally. Because despite the many positive conversations my books have engendered around cultural taboos like skipping baby showers and hating on Iceland — I still get radio show hosts, podcasters, and random strangers slipping into my DMs telling me that being selfish is the one thing with which they just can't get on board.

The resistance is strong in this one.

I understand. "Don't be selfish" has been drilled into us since we were kids hanging out in the communal sandbox, where "selfishness" meant hurting others, or only helping ourselves at others' expense.

Our parents told us not to be selfish with our toys. Other kids' parents told our parents to tell us not to be selfish with our toys. And if we acted selfish anyway, we got scolded. We also may have gotten bonked in the face with the Nerf water gun we were trying to yank back from the kid who thought it was okay to "share" our brand-new birthday present before we had a chance to break it our damn selves.

**We were taught that sharing was caring, and, conversely, that *not* sharing was *not* caring**—that if we didn't give of our toys, freely and without restriction, we were being "bad." And this is a good, simple lesson for youngsters who are just getting familiar with the social contract, but it shouldn't obligate us to give of OURSELVES without restriction, always and forever.

We're adults now. We understand nuance. And if you try to go through the sandbox of life **being *completely* selfless and *never* selfish,** you'll wind up buried up to your neck with zero toys, watching other kids have all the fun. (Which, I might add, leaves you wide open for a bonking.)

So with all due respect to the people who raised us, it's high time to move this particular line in the sand. I intend to do it with sound logic, shrewd reasoning, and a little help from Vanilla Ice.

# You can't please everyone, so you've got to please yourself

Ricky Nelson sang it all the way to the Top 40 back in 1972 and GIRL WAS NOT WRONG. You will never be able to please everyone. There will always be someone who thinks you should go to parties you don't want to attend, spend eighteen years raising (not to mention thirteen hours squeezing out) a descendant you don't want, or share your Pizza Hut personal pan pizza just because your friend foolishly experimented with the Tuscani® Chicken Alfredo Pasta and now regrets her life choices.

When this version of Judgy McJudgerson pops up on your radar and says "Don't be so selfish," he's really saying:

"Don't turn down an invite to your buddy's out-of-state Sigma Chi reunion just because you have a better use for the five hundred dollars you'd have to spend on airfare and hotel."

"Don't deprive the planet of an eight billionth person just because you don't feel like nurturing it (or having your vagina/abdomen torn asunder)."

"Don't eat the dinner you were excited about just because Diana insists on 'trying new things.'"

And he MIGHT AS WELL be saying:

"Don't be so happy."

In all of these cases, you've established what you want others to do unto you—that is, let you manage your money and your reproductive system the way you like, and enjoy your meal free from vultures. And presumably you'd be willing to do the same unto them, because you're not so fucking judgy. You're not the one in violation of the Golden Rule here.

What does Judgy McJudgerson have against you

being happy? Well, maybe his version of happiness doesn't match up with yours. Maybe *he's* not happy and he wants some company. (Misery loves it, you know.) Maybe Judgy does not get as aroused by a personal pan pizza as you do. Who knows? But as long as you're not being an asshole, an insufferable prick, or a psychopath, who cares?

**Knowing, asking for, pursuing, and preserving what makes you happy may be selfish. But it's also smart.**

---

### SPF Happy

The mental block that a lot of people have against being selfish arises because we think of selfishness in terms of taking away from others. So instead, let's think about it in terms of preserving our own well-being. Do you wear a seat belt in the car? Sunscreen at the beach? Do you go to sleep when you're tired and drink water when you're thirsty? If the answer is yes to any/all of these, then you're already a pro at protecting your own self-interests! You *have* to be selfish about this stuff, because unless you're an infant or a billionaire with manservants attending to your every whim, nobody else is responsible for doing it for you. And the same goes for protecting your happiness. It's wonderful to have relationships with friends, family, and partners where you make each other happy—but all I'm saying is, if you forget to put on sunblock, whose fault is it that you got burned?

---

The fact is, Judgy McJudgerson and the Selfish Police are going to get on your case no matter what. It's just who they are—we all grew up in the same sandbox, and they haven't grown out of it. But while they're busy patrolling the perimeter, you're busy reading this book and getting on with your life.

Ricky Nelson was right. You can't please everyone, so why not start by pleasing yourself?

Oh, and if I were you, I'd get started on that today, because the thing about pleasing yourself is, **you never know how much longer you might have to do it.**

## Everybody dies

I'm guessing my editor read the title of this section and reflexively reached for his iPhone to email me about "starting Part II on a lighter note," but listen, Mike, Ricky Nelson's private plane didn't go down in flames on New Year's Eve 1985 so that we could all be squeamish about mortality. Bear with me for a sec—I'm gearing up to make one of those excellent points you're so fond of.

Death is the great equalizer. It happens to all of us and there are no do-overs.* To my mind, that means every hour should be spent "living life to its fullest" and "seizing the day" and other goals that belong on cheesy motivational posters, not in a cheekily profane book of unconventional wisdom.

My version of that poster would look like this:

---

* Unless you believe in reincarnation, which I don't, though if possible I would greatly enjoy coming back as a lizard so I could lie on a hot rock all day doing nothing.

Move over, Paulo Coelho!

Listen, I know it's morbid, but with so many possibilities, choices, and outcomes, not to mention other people's opinions to deal with—and only one chance to navigate them, which might last another fifty years or only another five minutes—**thinking about death helps me focus my energy on living the best life I can.**

I was six years old the first time someone I knew died. She was five—my cousin Emily, who had been born with cystic fibrosis. Although she spent much of her short life in the hospital, she was cheerful and giggly in the face of her incurable disease. Seeing her coffin at the front of the church as her father, my uncle Bob, delivered her eulogy, is one of my earliest memories.

In December of 2016, Bob died of a heart attack at the age of sixty-seven. This time it was me delivering a eulogy.

The intervening thirty years have been marked by funerals for grandparents, aunts, uncles, neighbors, and friends. A couple of months ago, I found out via Facebook that my first boyfriend had died suddenly at forty-four. So many of my peers have already said goodbye to their parents, and some have suffered the untimely loss of siblings, spouses, and even children.

So whenever I'm wrestling with asking for what I want or saying no to something I don't, I remind myself that unlike many people I've known and loved, I'm lucky to have a choice in the matter, and that I ought to use it wisely.

Death is tragic and devastating, but at least the person who's dying gets relief when the lights go out and the last synapse fires. Peace out. Game over. No time left on the clock for regrets. Whereas those of us left behind have all *kinds* of time to tangle with the encroaching hordes of fear and regret and what-ifs triggered by a brush with someone else's death.

Or maybe, like Emily and Uncle Bob, we don't have much time at all.

Do you see where I'm going with this? If your starring role on earth is a limited run — and I hate to break it to you, but it surely is — **why impose limits on the happiness you can have while you're still here?**

# "You keep using that word. I do not think it means what you think it means."

Okay, enough morbidity. (But thanks for indulging me, Mike. You're a mensch!) It's time to talk semantics — because every contract has a loophole, and far be it from me not to find and exploit it on my readers' behalf.

So riddle me this:

The fine folks at Merriam-Webster insist that being selfish means being **"concerned excessively or exclusively with oneself"** and **"without regard for others."** Well, sure, if we take this definition at face value, then I see why many people are not yet convinced that being selfish is *ever* okay. It sounds pretty bad — on par with "smells like Roquefort" or "kicks puppies" in terms of Stuff You Don't Want People Saying About You. Definitely in or close to psychopath territory, which is no good. You know how I feel about psychopaths.

But despite what "people" who write "dictionaries" would have you believe, **when it comes to selfishness, there is a whole MOTHERFUCKING GAMUT between good and bad.**

It encompasses "taking care of your own needs first and *then* having plenty of regard for others" as well as "taking care of yourself when it has absolutely zero impact, positive or negative, on anyone else at all."

| GOOD SELFISH | BAD SELFISH |
|---|---|
| Making sure you get 8 hours of sleep so you can be bright-eyed and bushy-tailed for your family | Falling asleep on the couch and expecting your family to tiptoe around you for eight hours |
| Handling the group cupcake order—to be nice, *and* so you know you'll get what you want | Ordering six dozen of your favorite flavor and no one else's |
| Waking up early to get the best lounge chair at your hotel pool | Leaving your towel draped across three chairs and going back to bed for two hours |
| Putting on your oxygen mask before helping others | Bogarting someone else's oxygen mask |

I've said it before and I'll say it again: **Being selfish is not always a bad thing.** This shouldn't be so controversial.

Being concerned about yourself doesn't exclude you from ALSO being generous, caring, attentive, and empathetic toward others. It might even be what ENABLES you to be those things. (Remember what happened when I selfishly skipped all those marketing meetings to catch up on my beauty sleep? I tell ya what, I was a goddamn *peach* to be around for the rest of the day.)

**The good kind of selfish is simply self-care**—a concept that's been fueling billion-dollar industries, selling magazines, and giving Gwyneth Paltrow something to do for many years. They've figured it out; why shouldn't you?

**And sometimes you even *need* to be selfish *in order to* help other people**—like when you put on your oxygen mask first before assisting others. We're no good to one another passed out from $O_2$ deprivation, and that's an FAA-mandated FACT.

### 7 ways you being selfish can benefit others

1. If you selfishly run home to binge-watch *House of Cards* instead of going to an after-work mixer, that's half a bottle more free Pinot Grigio for your coworkers.
2. If you selfishly commandeer the radio station on a family road trip, you're saving everyone from your dad's boner for Andy Borowitz on NPR *Weekend Edition*.
3. If you selfishly set the DVR to record *Top Chef* instead of *Pawn Stars,* you're protecting your roommate from the misguided notion that his grandma's old brass fireplace pokers are worth enough to cover his rent.
4. If you selfishly choose not to provide your parents with a grandbaby to smother, you are also saving the whole world 5.7 times what would otherwise be your lifetime carbon dioxide emissions. Go green!
5. If you selfishly decline to run in the three-legged race at your kid's school fundraiser, you're saving Marcy's mom from an ankle sprain and ripped capris.
6. If you selfishly dress your dog, Avon Barksdale, in a pink raincoat and matching booties because YOU think it's adorable, he will have YOU to thank for keeping him dry while pooping in inclement weather.
7. If you selfishly take a corner piece from the brownie pan, you're showing at least three other people it's okay to take one too. Lead by example, friend.

Judgy can call me selfish all he wants, but I know I'm doing it *while also* having regard for others. I may be turning down birthday party invites because I'm "excessively concerned" with budgeting my time, but that's in the service of finishing this book and helping YOU feel good about doing the same.*

At the end of the day, I have absolutely no problem (a) being excessively concerned with my own self-interest and (b) admitting it.

You can be selfish and feel good about it too, if you put your mind to it. Here are three tips to get you started:

### Attract your opposite

I'm sure there are parents who would describe themselves as "morning people," and for whom having an extra hour to themselves later in the day — before the kids get home from school — is when they feel most #blessed. If you, a non-Morning Person, feel shamed by the Selfish Police into volunteering for the a.m. car pool slot, you've not only deprived yourself of an hour

---

* Sorry, John; sorry, Sitso. Happy belated!

of sleep, you've actually done a *disservice* to Morning Person Parent, who is now stuck with the 3 p.m. run—aka just about the time his or her breakfast power smoothie has worn off. This is what we call a "lose-lose." You need to find the yin to your yang and then JOIN FORCES! Guilt-free afternoon pickups for you, and those inveterate early birds can take first shift to gain some freedom later in the day. (And Judgy can snack on it.)

**Break new ground**

Tradition is the enemy of selfishness, because tradition allows generations past to make decisions on your behalf. You don't even get a say in it, let alone the chance to be "concerned excessively" with yourself. You just have to show up at a *Dirty Dancing*-esque cabin in the woods for a week every July because that's how your parents did it, and their parents before them. Well, now you're an adult with a burgeoning gnocchi habit and a preference for the Amalfi coast over the Catskills, so perhaps it's time to start your own tradition that other people can be annoyed by. This is what we call "quid pro quo." But you're not a monster, remember? So while you're creating your new tradition of Spending My Time Off as I See Fit, you could *involve* your family in it by adding a tradition of Bringing Back an Alcoholic Souvenir to Improve Relations at Christmas.

## Your absence is their present

I'm a huge fan of the can't-make-it-but-send-a-gift school of RSVP'ing, which accomplishes two things at once: I don't have to do something I don't want to do, and the host gets a bottle of nice champagne or a set of superhero onesies or a box of frozen Williams-Sonoma croissants, which are THE BEST. So yeah, maybe I couldn't be at your retirement party, but you didn't have to shell out $49.99 for my three-course dinner at the Elks' Lodge *and* you got a Wooly Bugger, a Stimulator, and a Gold Ribbed Hare's Ear out of the deal.* I also tend to be more generous when I can't make it to an event than if I were spending the time/energy/money to go, *plus* bringing a gift. Some-

---

* Those are all very famous fly-fishing lures. Get your mind out of the gutter.

body's nephews and nieces are gonna do real well on the bar and bat mitzvah checks.

Honestly, there are so many more good reasons to embrace selfishness, I wish I could experience the profound joy of doing it for the first time. I'm jealous, you guys. Have fun.

## Selflessness: the mother of all myths

Finally, since we're on this topic, and since this is what anti-gurus are for, I'm going to expose some gray area when it comes to being self*less,* too, which our friends at Merriam-Webster define as **"having no concern for self."**

No concern. None. Zip, zilch, nada.

I ask you, does that sound sustainable? Maybe if your name is Mother Teresa, but do you really want her life? (If you really want her life, you are reading the wrong book.)

And anyway, it's entirely possible to do and be good in the world without committing your entire existence to the self-defeating — and often self-harming — concept of having *no concern whatsoever for yourself.*

Take a different mother, for example: mine. If you knew Sandi, you'd probably think of her when the word "selfless" gets bandied about. Need a ride? She'll be there in a jiff. Hungry? Tuna sandwich, coming right up. Does your core temperature run ridiculously hot, to the point that you require air conditioning in December? No worries, she'll go put on a third sweater.

Is my mom selfless? Yep! Mostly.

But even while displaying more than her share of concern for others, she's still looking out for her own self-interest on a daily basis. She sleeps in when she could *theoretically* be making somebody breakfast. Communes with Jack Reacher — rugged assassin and star of Lee Child's globally bestselling thriller franchise — when my dad is right there on the couch next to her and could easily be engaged in conversation. Refuses to go easy on me in Words with Friends when she knows how much her only daughter, her firstborn, the flesh of her flesh, *hates* losing at that infernally addictive game.

*"No concern for self,"* my ass, Mother.

The point is, those pockets of selfishness — aka self-care — don't negate her otherwise selfless behavior. She needs a little recharging if she's going to keep up with all those good deeds and tuna sandwiches she's so famous for.

By the same token, my usual focus on surrounding

myself with peace and quiet doesn't mean I would *never* babysit for a friend in need. (I'll have you know, I've done that twice.)

**Purely selfish people? Monsters, one and all. But purely self*less* people don't have it so good either.**

Sure, they might win a Nobel Peace Prize every once in a while, but they also wind up bankrolling their adult children, going to prison for their bosses' transgressions, and being eaten first by fellow shipwreck survivors. *They* are the reason they can't have nice things.

Why not come hang out in the motherfucking gamut with Sandi and me? It's quite lovely this time of year.

# I learned it by watching Vanilla Ice

The preceding arguments in favor of selfishness may take some getting used to. You have to let go of a lifetime of conditioning and also be willing to take my word against the dictionary. I believe you can do it. But if you're struggling with accepting selfishness as a good, useful quality and/or deploying it with confidence, I want to leave you with a little something extra to sustain you in your darkest hours.

Unfortunately I'm not [yet] authorized to go around making up words that get officially adopted by the entire English-speaking world. My agent is working on it. But for the purposes of closing this semantic loophole I've been fondling for the last few pages, allow me to at least offer you a new spin on an old one.

It involves a tiny tweak, similar to how one Robert Matthew "Vanilla Ice" Van Winkle tweaked Queen and David Bowie's number one hit "Under Pressure" to create "Ice Ice Baby."* My solution, like Vanilla Ice's, makes life easier on all of us. Nobody has to learn a whole new word (or bassline); instead, we can just put the emphasis on a different syllable and go on about our day.

It's like this: If you're tired of Judgy McJudgerson calling you selfish when you act in a way that benefits you WHILE looking out for others (or that doesn't adversely impact others at all) — just tell him it's actually pronounced self-ISH, and you sure are, loud and proud, thank you very much!

---

* "We sampled it from them but it's not the same bassline. It goes 'ding ding ding di di ding ding…ding ding ding di di ding ding.' That's the way theirs goes. Ours goes 'ding ding ding di di ding ding…DING… ding ding ding di di ding ding.'" — Vanilla Ice on MTV, 1990

> Selfish (adj.) [pronounced self-ISH]: looking out for
> yourself while also not being an asshole, an
> insufferable prick, or a psychopath.

In other words, and per the examples on pages 76–79:

If it's self-ISH to let other moms volunteer for morning car pool duty because you don't function well before 8 a.m. — but you take the afternoon run off their hands so they can get their *Ellen* on — then so be it.

If it's self-ISH to use your summer vacation days on a solo trip to Italy instead of upholding a tired family Fourth of July tradition — but you show up on Christmas with bottles of duty-free grappa for everyone — then so be it.

If it's self-ISH to turn down a party invitation because you don't want to go out or you're too busy with other things — but you send a nice gift to honor the occasion — then so be it.

And if being self-ISH results in you being a happier, calmer, more generous individual—then so be it.

Checkmate, Merriam-Webster.

# Third time's the charm

To recap: In *The Life-Changing Magic of Not Giving a Fuck,* I focused on learning how to give fewer, better fucks by saying no—an act that is frequently perceived as selfish when "no" is not the answer the person on the other end wants to hear. And sure, if you say it in a jerky or poorly thought-out way, it can qualify as "bad." That's why you use the NotSorry Method. Honest and polite. **Prioritize your needs, but don't be an asshole about it.**

See, you're taking their feelings into consideration! Not entirely selfish.

In *Get Your Shit Together,* I pressed the issue yet further, explaining how to—yes, selfishly—strategize your time and focus your energy to maximize what you get out of the fucks you *do* still give (including the all-important "me time" fucks).

**The by-product of getting your own life under control is that you BECOME a more present, able, kind, and happy person for everyone else.**

Again, since it benefits others, it's not purely selfish after all.

Here in *You Do You*, I pulled out the big guns: death and wordplay. You want to accidentally fall through a manhole tomorrow and break your neck without having eaten that corner brownie piece? I thought not. And okay, fine, it's bad to be selfish (pronounced SELF-ish). STOP COMING AT ME, BRO.

Being self-ISH, on the other hand...well, I think I've made a pretty compelling case. And they're homonyms, so nobody has to work too hard. You're welcome.

I do hope this finally closes the book on the whole selfish conversation, because I have other things to write about and other controversial ideas to disseminate. (If you're reading this and you have a radio show, just wait until you get to my thoughts on "putting family first" in Part IV.)

For now, onward, to the perils of being perfect!

# Do Your Best<sup>*</sup>

*Except when you can't. Or you don't
want to. Or it's giving you heartburn.*

"I have a question for you," I said to my husband.

"Yes, dear?"

"It's a serious question. Like, this isn't a joke, and I'm also not criticizing you—I really want to know the answer."

He folded his hands in his lap, regarding me with the practiced gaze of a man who has been in a relationship with a perfectionist for nearly two decades.

"I'm curious"—I hesitated, sincerely not wanting to come off as critical, but desperate for answers—"if… when you hang up the bath towel…do you look at it and think *That's straight*, or do you notice that you left it crooked and you just don't care? Or do you…could you possibly…"

"What do you think?" he responded, one eyebrow raised, cool as an Old Spice model.

"You don't even notice, do you?"

"Got it in one."

✼ ✻ ✺

"The Towel Conversation" is illustrative of three things: my mild OCD; the way my husband and I sometimes see the world differently; and how we choose to interact with it. For example, I was a straight-A student because B-pluses gave me stomach aches; he happily brought home B-minuses because that was the minimum he had to hit in order to keep his parents off his back. I am very careful and precise in both word and deed; he's more of a shoot-first-ask-questions-later bull in a china shop. I beat myself up over the smallest failures; he rolls with the punches.

Sure, I've had success in my life, and sure, much of it has come as a result of all that hard work, focus, and discipline. Also a fair amount of privilege and some actual perfection, like that one time I made a soufflé. (Quit while you're ahead, kids!) But I've also experienced a lot of self-inflicted disappointment as a result of the same. **I've overachieved, but also underperformed — and if I hadn't always put so much pressure on myself to succeed, it wouldn't have been quite so crushing to come up short.** (The sleepless night I once endured after misspelling "Hemingway" on a high school paper, thereby receiving a grade of 97 instead of 100, was a low point.)

---

### 5 reasons why it's bad to be perfect

1. You'll never get to live out your fantasy of staying late to get "tutoring help" from the hot professor.
2. Your friends will expect you to host ALL THE PARTIES and provide ALL THE SOUFFLÉS.
3. Your Uber rating has nowhere to go but down.
4. You won't get picked for a one-on-one wardrobe consultation from a celebrity stylist on *Ambush Makeover*.
5. You are doomed to spend the majority of your day wanting to punch other people in the face because nobody lives up to your inhuman standards.

---

The Towel Conversation took place a few years ago, before I became what I am now — a recovering perfectionist. Today, I'm here on the other side (or more accurately, somewhere in the middle) to tell you that **doing your best all the time and trying to be Perfect with a capital P isn't all it's cracked up to be.**

In fact, you know what?

# FUCK PERFECT.

There, I said it.

It takes courage to admit that you are both flawed and vulnerable, and **being courageous is better than being perfect** any day of the week and twice on Sunday. Accepting that we all have flaws — and therefore, vulnerabilities — is the only way forward into gaining confidence in who and what we are.

**Acceptance breeds confidence.**

And you don't have to be a natural-born perfectionist like *moi* to feel pressured to "do your best" on a daily basis. It's a chorus we've all heard during every tee-ball game we've ever played, before every test we've ever taken, at every job we've ever had, and in advance of every elimination challenge we've ever seen on *Top Chef.* The people yelling or advising or even just gently suggesting it weren't necessarily trying to fuck with our heads in perpetuity (they may not even have equated our "best" with "actual perfection"), but the pressure builds nonetheless.

*Do your best. Be the best. Don't mess up.*

That shit'll catch up with you if you let it. It certainly caught up with me, and now I've got a monkey on my back for life. I named him Ernest.

We have some advice for you.

# What would Marty McFly do?

Once I became a self-help "expert," people started asking me, "If you could go back in time, what would you tell your younger self?"

My answer is always the same: **"You don't have to be perfect."**

(Though if I could give my younger self a second piece of advice, it would be, "In fifteen years, that $29 tongue piercing is going to cost you $700 in dental work, so you might wanna reconsider this decision.")

Unfortunately, we don't live in a Robert Zemeckis movie, so Young Me will never receive Future Me's hard-won counsel on the dangers of perfectionism and metal mouth jewelry. But I bet that Current You could benefit from at least one of these lessons, so I've taken the liberty of drafting a letter.

Feel free to tear it out and mount it in your locker, cubicle, or bathroom, or inside your underwear drawer — wherever you're likely to see it on a daily basis. (I really hope you open your underwear drawer on a daily basis, BTW.) And do share it with anyone else in your life who loses sleep over their GCSEs, their colleagues' opinions, or being the glue that holds an entire team together.

Dear Young Me,

Doing your best — performing to your maximum capacity, always — is not sustainable. You're going to have bad days and slow days and hungover days, and if you beat yourself up over all of them and don't allow yourself time to recuperate, you're going to be in for a rude awakening one day in oh, say, 1997.

**Lesson #1: Slack off every once in a while, or someday, you will ruin Christmas.**

Barely a semester into your freshman year of college, you will get sick. It will start as a common cold, sinus infection–type thing, and despite your burning forehead and throbbing glands, you will soldier on. You will show up for every class and do all the reading and turn the papers in on time. You will remain convinced that it's possible to get straight A's at one of the country's premier universities just like you did at your tiny public school in the thirty-ninth-largest state in the union. You will keep setting your alarm in the morning and studying late into the night. (You'll also HANDWRITE all of your English lit essays before typing them up, because computers are still new to you and you're a glutton for punishment.)

Eventually, for several days following your eighteenth birthday, you will find yourself flat on your back in your single dorm bed with a golf ball–sized lump in your neck and your new college friends stopping by with store-brand OJ and worried looks in their eyes.

You'll never get a diagnosis, though Older You thinks it's safe to assume that a combination of stress, toxins, and sleep deprivation was the culprit, and the cure was to go home to the thirty-ninth-largest state in the union for the holidays and lie flat on your back some more until that gross neck thing went away. (Your relatives had to pretend they weren't looking at your bulge. You could barely hold your nog. It wasn't pretty.)

So please note: Clinging tight to the highest standards until your body stages a feverish, mucus-filled revolt — is nobody's idea of a *joyeux Noël*. Seriously, even Jesus took a break on Sundays, and people worship the ground that guy walks on.

**Lesson #2: Perfection is in the eye of the beholder.**

Three years later, when you are twenty-one—fresh off of graduation, your first job, and your first round of start-up layoffs—you will work on the ground floor of a gloomy, cigarette smoke–filled town house on the Upper East Side of New York City for a lady who rarely has anything nice to say to or about anybody. She's a tough nut to crack, but you'll make it your personal mission to wow her with your brilliance, your unparalleled work ethic, and your unimpeachable instincts for improving her fifty-year-old business practices.

You are convinced you will be the BEST assistant she has ever had.

Against rather tall odds, everything will be going well until one random day when you make an innocent comment for which she will—almost gleefully—berate you. You will (to your horror) start crying right in front of her, and as she's climbing the stairs to her smoky lair, she will turn around and say, "I'm glad you're crying, because it shows that you're human."

You will realize that this woman had regarded you as some kind of automaton. You were always Sarah-on-the-spot—yet far from pleasing her, it actually raised her hackles. Because as a world-weary seventysomething, she knew that NOBODY IS PERFECT, least of all a nervy little twentysomething with a Harvard degree and a bunch of big ideas. So the moment you said something that could possibly be twisted to engage her legendary temper, she pounced—and you were blindsided because of your own naïve belief that she couldn't possibly ever find any fault with you.

Well, guess what? You can study and strive and genuflect all you want, but that's not going to stop a professor from grading your essay subjectively, a team member from taking credit for your work, or your boss from serving you your ass on a platter, whether you deserve it or not.

**Lesson #3: Damn, it feels good to be a gangster.**

This'll cheer you up. One time when you are about twenty-seven, a highly respected senior member of your business will accuse you via phone of being "the worst fucking editor [he's] ever worked with," and you will promptly hang up on him. When he calls back and tells your assistant he wants to "offer an olive branch," you will not only not take his call, you will never speak to him again.

**Lesson #4: Stop and smell your new business cards.**

As the years go by, ambition will continue to be a guiding force in your life. That's not a terrible thing all by itself, but when you get promoted, instead of pausing to enjoy the improved view, you'll have already set your sights a few rungs higher up the ladder. You'll have exciting and commendable successes, but the glow never lasts long before you're itching to outdo yourself.

A smart person will one day tell you this is called "hedonic adaptation," but you just call it "my late twenties and early thirties."

It's like those "personal bests" runners are always posting on Facebook, cogs in a vicious cycle of Never Enough. Achieving a personal best means that what they did *last* time — which was at that point their "best" — was not good enough for them, so they kept pushing to improve it. Ergo, they are NEVER SATISFIED.

Of course, there's much to be said in favor of self-improvement, but if your best is *never* good enough, then what good is it? (You're no ultramarathoner, but this lesson will come in handy when you write a few very popular self-help books and yet Oprah seems to have permanently misplaced your number.)

**Lesson #5: Dial back on the "git 'er done." It's good for you and keeps everyone else on their toes.**

This is something you'll figure out on your own pretty early on, but it's worth reiterating for anyone else who may be reading this letter, of whom Future You hopes there are several hundred thousand:

Know that while you're busy perfecting your *modus operandi,* other people will notice.

And start taking advantage of you.

These people will see that you are an unstoppable machine of excellence and they will, consciously or unconsciously, begin depending on you to prop them up. It happens to you in school when other kids crane their necks to copy off your paper, and it'll happen to you at jobs and within friendships. If you were to someday join a prison gang, you would be in the gym every day and your rivals would keep dropping weight, knowing you would keep adding it to your metaphorical barbell until you were crushed by your own awesomeness.

Anyway, what I'm saying, Young Me, is don't join a prison gang. But also that doing your best can be exhausting enough without doing everyone else's best while you're at it. (Plus, it's fun to watch people squirm when they haven't done the reading.) How about we let them do *their* goddamn best for a change?

Well, that's it for now, kiddo. I hope you'll take these lessons to heart. Although if you do, I guess that means a lot of the events I've described will never come to pass and you might not wind up writing this book in 2017, which means Future You can't actually teach you the lessons, which means…it's a very good thing we don't live in a Robert Zemeckis movie. So yeah, you're a little bit screwed in your teens and twenties, but what doesn't kill us makes us bestselling anti-gurus who can help a lot more people on the back end, which isn't such a bad outcome.

Love,
Future You

PS No matter how much time you spend straightening the bath towels, your future husband or your future houseguests or your future cat are just going to fuck them up anyway. Relax.

# Okay, but *how* do I relax???

Past me doesn't have a prayer, but here are a few concrete things Current You (and Current Me, for that matter) can do to ratchet down the Perfect-O-Meter in our daily lives:

### Lower the bar

One of my favorite tips is inspired by celebrity chef and all-around goddess Ina Garten, who says that when planning a dinner party, she writes out the whole menu in advance and then cuts one or two dishes before she even goes grocery shopping. Voilà! Life just got easier. I feel like we could all learn a thing or two about quality of life from a woman who goes by "The Barefoot Contessa."

### Look around you

The world is full of dumbasses. If your company hasn't gone under yet with Jim, Allison, and Talia over there heading up the advertising department, it's probably okay for you to take a three-day weekend.

## Be the first to fuck shit up

The day my father got a brand-new 1987 Nissan Maxima, he took us all out to get ice cream. We ate it in the car so that if anything was going to happen to that sweet, sweet brown suede interior, it was going to happen right away and then my dad could stop torturing himself with imagined horrors. Know thyself.

## Talk to literally any old person

Old people have been through it all, y'all. They know shit happens. They know there's no point in being perfect. They're just happy to be here, which you should be too.

It's pretty simple, really: Whether it's in your nature or just on your agenda for any given day, **don't let doing your best get in the way of living your best life.** You can work hard at the things that matter and aim high if it makes you happy, but if you fall short, that's okay. **Remember your WNDs.** I'm quite sure you neither WANT nor NEED a peptic ulcer, and we all DESERVE to cut ourselves some slack every once in a while.

In fact, Ernest told me he'd appreciate it if you brought the standards down a little for the rest of us. He could use a break too.

# Don't Be Difficult<sup>*</sup>

*Ask for what you want, push back on
what you don't, and beware
the focus group.*

Many folks would rather turn the other cheek than go against the grain, rub anyone the wrong way, or make waves. That's understandable. It gets tiring being on the front lines of "Jesus fucking Christ!" all day long. Other folks put in half the effort — they get up on their high horse over some stuff, but when challenged, they crumple like an origami swan in a Jacuzzi.*

Those folks are not me. Perhaps they are not you, either.

If you're like me, you know that being "difficult" means being confident and vocal, challenging ourselves

---

* Another legally protected trademark, for the generic term "hot tub bath."

and others, and standing up for what we believe in—
even if that means taking an unpopular stance or one that
puts us squarely in the crosshairs of "YOU again?"

It could be in the workplace—defending your unconventional ideas, high standards, or entrepreneurial spirit
to less-than-like-minded colleagues.

It could be at home—when you decide this family
needs to start eating healthy, goddammit, so you put Ben
and Jerry on lockdown.

Or it could be on a lengthy FaceTime call with your
mother during which you patiently explain that Aunt
Cindy is no longer invited to your home because she's
a bitter old racist, and you don't care if that makes it
hard for Mom to decide where to spend Rosh Hashanah
this year.

In any event, I feel like you and I have reached the
point in our relationship where I can be blunt. So here
goes: **I am sick and fucking tired of people who
don't *understand* me telling me that *I'm* the one who's
difficult.**

Whether it's at work, in relationships, or at restau-
rants where I really meant it when I asked for that steak

well done, why should I earn demerits — or nasty looks, eye rolls, melodramatic sighs, or spit in my condiments — for having a strong, clear, LEGITIMATE position and asserting it?

If this kind of stuff constitutes "being difficult," then sign me up! (Though I would mentally redecorate that phrase to say "acting bullish in pursuit of things I want" and "holding others to the same standard I hold myself" as well as "remaining grossed out by undercooked meat.")

Additionally, when challenged on such legitimate positions, I resent Judgy McJudgerson's assessment that I'm the one who should soften, mellow, or completely blunt my edges to suit the narrow view of a vanilla majority; or that I should give up on my needs and desires so someone else — a classmate, a coworker, a line cook — can have an "easier" time of it.

What's that, you say? *Me too?* Excellent. Let's take that righteous indignation and run with it.

# Being difficult: the spectrum

The difference between me and, say, the person who thinks I'm being difficult by sending back a too-rare steak that I ordered well done is that *I* understand that some *other* people like their meat bloody, and would therefore understand if *those* people sent back an overcooked filet and requested, you know, what they actually ordered. (I don't make it a habit to send back food — I truly don't — but this is an easy, universal example of what happens when you want what you want, you don't get it, and unless you push back, your happiness is at steak. Er, stake.)

---

### Just the tip

I've always said you can get away with a lot if you're the kind of person who sends regular thank-you notes, and tipping well is the same idea. Not violently shoving hundred-dollar bills in a waiter's mouth like estranged Kardashian in-law Scott Disick, mind you, but adding a few percentage points when you know your requests might have been a little out of the ordinary. Yes, the customer is always right, but the customer does not have to be a Disick about it.

---

As for you? Well, Judgy might label you "difficult" for calling out your colleagues on bad behavior, or for speaking your mind at a PTA meeting. Maybe you're guilty of defending a blue state opinion at a red state holiday party, or requesting a change to your friend Anne's rehearsal dinner seating arrangement because you slept with her cousin five years ago after her graduation party and you're gunning for a repeat. (She doesn't know that, which is why she thinks you're being "difficult," not "a horndog.")

Congratulations, you're difficult! But legitimately so. (And in the case of Anne's friend, you are also self-ISH, but we've been over that.)

**There is nothing wrong with liking things the way you like them and asking for what you want.**

There is also nothing wrong with aggressively pursuing what you want when it lies outside the bounds of what other people approve of or feel like dealing with. In fact, I think you should be commended for having the courage of your convictions, standing up for what's right, and taking charge of your sex life. (Just wait until *after* Anne's rehearsal dinner to seal the deal, 'kay?)

You're even allowed to press your "difficult" agenda

forward when it might seem ridiculous to everyone around you but in point of fact is *hurting* no one — per Meg-Ryan-as-Sally-Albright ordering pie à la mode.

**Just don't go around being difficult FOR THE HELL OF IT.** Tormenting others as a form of pure entertainment is never okay. Put the lotion in the basket and walk away, Buffalo Bill.

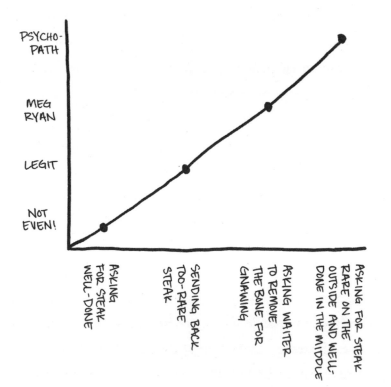

# How to be "difficult"

Now let's say you have some "difficult" urges that you recognize but haven't been acting on, because you're a good little rule-follower whose ability to smile and nod in the face of other people's bullshit would be legendary if they ever realized you were doing it. (Instead, they just think you're "one of them.") As a result, you're not as deep into the spectrum as you'd like to be, and you're wondering what you can do to get there.

Wonder no more.

Herewith, a primer on the twin pillars of being difficult: **asking for what you want** and **pushing back on what you don't.**

## You don't get what you don't ask for.

Requesting something different than what's on offer is a perfectly reasonable thing to do. You probably shouldn't go all Meg Ryan *every* time you go out to dinner (unless you really enjoy the flavor profile of someone else's saliva added to your halibut), but you also don't have to **constantly settle for less than you want, need, or deserve** in the course of an average day.

The worst thing that can happen when you ask for something is that the askee says no. And if they say no for a stupid reason, then you can and should ask again (see: *I'll be in my office*). In *Get Your Shit Together,* I addressed this issue specifically as it relates to getting a raise or a promotion at work — literally asking your boss "What do I have to do to get you to give me what I want?"

Well, the same principle applies to getting *anything* your little heart desires or deserves. Just ask. For example:

**Help around the apartment from your roommates.** They seem to think it's easier to live in filth than to wipe their Sriracha rings off the countertop once a week, but requesting a standard of communal living that surpasses "bus terminal Panda Express" doesn't even make you difficult — it makes you an adult without a roach problem.

**The best a hotel has to offer.** Several hundred rooms at the same price do not equal several hundred rooms at the same experience. Why not ask for a southern exposure; a corner room with no neighbors; to be on the interior vs. street side; or to be closer to (or farther from) the elevator, whatever your preference? It takes five more minutes on the reservationist's end to accommodate such requests, and it could mean a better view or night's sleep for you, so why not? You may be difficult, but you're also practical.

**Good seats at the movie theater.** There's nothing I hate more than showing up late to the movies and getting stuck with shitty seats. This is why I refuse to meet certain friends outside the theater, because if they get hung up at work and I end up with a front-row, neck-craning spot for *Tropic Thunder 2,** I will spend two hours getting progressively more angry, resentful, and cross-eyed. (This is also why some friends won't agree to meet *me* outside the theater, because I insist on arriving forty-five minutes before previews. Suit yourselves, but at least we'll still BE friends when the show's over.)

---

* This is me asking the Universe to make *Tropic Thunder 2.*

**A fresh personal pan pizza at the Domino's in the Santo Domingo airport.** Hey, the ones under the heat lamp looked like they'd been sitting there for hours. It's not as though the gentleman behind the counter had anything better to do than make me a freshie, so I asked. (Actually, I made my husband ask, because his Spanish is better than mine.)\*

**Appointments at your convenience.** Did you know you don't have to take the first slot they offer if it doesn't suit your preferences? Unless your acupuncturist is moving to Australia or your dentist is only open on Tuesdays and every other slot is taken, there's no reason to settle for 8 a.m. (if you're a later sleeper), noon (if you hate skipping lunch), or 5:30 (if you're worried about getting stuck in rush hour traffic). The date and time the receptionist gives you is probably just the first one that comes up in the book. If you find yourself thinking *I guess I could do that, but it'll mean getting up ass-early/low blood sugar for lunch/road rage for*

---

\* In case you're interested, the Spanish word for difficult is *difícil,* but the word for picky, *especial,* has a nicer ring to it, *especially* when your wife is listening.

*dinner*— DON'T SAY YES. Ask if they have anything else, or better yet, ask for a specific window, like only afternoons, or only Fridays. Does it create a little more work for the voice behind the phone? Sure, but the voice behind the phone gets paid for that.

**Better, more consistent orgasms.** Trust me, one "difficult" conversation with your partner about pacing and technique is worth far more than two in the bush.

---

### I'll be in my office

I once caused a boss to literally tear out her hair by asking for an office. I was a newly minted associate editor and naturally, I felt it was time I graduated from a cubicle to that small, windowless interior nook-with-a-door that nobody else was using anyway. I asked; she said she'd think about it. I waited a week and asked again; she told me, "Now is not a good time." I waited another week (still nobody using it; just a bunch of unattended boxes and an old jar of honey), asked again, and she yelled, "Sarah Knight, you are getting on my very last nerve!" while yanking at her scalp with both fists. But she finally told me I could have it. And that, munchkins, is how I got myself a door to close during the subsequent workplace crying jags that will factor later in this chapter.

## What a bargain!

So now that you've asked for what you want — you diffi-cult creature, you — it would behoove you to learn how to press for even more, and also how to push back on what you *don't* want. **That's where negotiating comes in.** This activity tends to brand those who engage in it as "diffi-cult," but if you don't value your time, energy, and money, who will?

Whether we're talking about your weeknight curfew, an extra personal day, or a better rate on a rental car, **once you get an answer, it's fine to ask whether the person on the other end can do better.**

And remember that negotiating works both ways — not only in terms of what you're getting, but of what you're *giving*. If people are asking too much of you, some-times you have to push back like a La-Z-Boy.

Below are some of my favorite tactics — ones that have gotten me everything from a better bottle of wine at the cheaper-bottle price, to a significant salary increase:

**Ask the questions you're not supposed to ask.** The social contract helps prevent us from making one another uncomfortable, which is great if you want to enjoy a unisex spa without anyone staring pointedly at your naughty bits. But in a negotiation, it's *useful* to make the other party flinch. For example, if you're trying to get more money out of your employer (and you suspect your colleague Dennis makes a LOT more than you for the same job), ask your boss straight out how much Dennis takes home, and whether you're worth less. You may get nowhere; you may get market information that's useful when you look for your next job; or you may get an *I like your style,* accompanied by a nice bump in pay. That's a lot of medium-bodied Oregon Pinot Noir.

**Lay down the law.** By trade, lawyers are tough negotiators, but you don't need a law qualification to take advantage of one of their favorite strategies: asking for more than you know you'd settle for. If you do that, the person on the other side can give a little without feeling like he lost (or you can look reasonable for "agreeing" to less than you originally demanded). This works in all kinds of scenarios, including non-business ones. Want your wife to go to that 49ers game with you on Thanksgiving? Ask for season tickets and negotiate down.

**Establish the precedent:** If you have a friend who asks a lot (read: too much) of you on a regular basis, you can reference the last thing she asked you to do with/for her when you respond to the next request. Something like, "Unfortunately since I left work early to go to your Pampered Chef party last week, I'm not going to be able to hit up your one-woman show at the Haha Hut on Tuesday." It's a little passive-aggressive, but so is Sheila.

**Shock and awe:** If your family thinks you're difficult because you have an inflexible "traveling with children" policy, then you could propose a deal: instead of agreeing to go on a Disney cruise this year for her sixth, you'll commit right now to taking your niece to Detroit to get her first tattoo when she turns sixteen. I bet you'll get a counteroffer.

**Take the shortcut:** I may be a decent negotiator, but I also despise inefficiency. If I don't have the time or desire to go back and forth on something, I just get comfortable with my own bottom line (and the fact that it might not get met), and then lay down an ultimatum, such as "I will pay [X amount] for the original codpiece worn by David Bowie in *Labyrinth* and not a penny more." If it doesn't work, then walk away, Renee. You might end up shelling out more than you technically *had* to, if you'd gone through a true negotiation, but you decided up front that a little more cash was worth a little less hassle. Sometimes, the person you're really negotiating with is you.

**Moral of the story: Don't be shy about getting the best deal for yourself that you can.** Heck, in many cultures, haggling is a way of life. Where I live in the Dominican Republic, if you don't bargain down the original price quoted then you are definitely, certainly, surely, *unquestionably* being ripped off. Negotiating may not work at an establishment that has firm prices (or, in the case of my father, on the curfew front), but there's wiggle room in a lot of life's transactions.

# Death by focus group

Now that I've helped cultivate your difficult streak, there's a particularly lousy by-product of LCD Living that I want to draw your attention to. I call it "death by focus group," and difficult people are the only ones who can prevent it.

As you probably know, the purpose of a focus group is to test a product or idea among a diverse group of consumers who have no skin in the game, in order to achieve a consensus about what works and what doesn't before the professionals (who do have game-skin) can implement and widely roll out that product or idea.

For example, if Lululemon wanted to find out whether their customers would go for a line of Misty Copeland–inspired workout gear that featured itchy neon tutus, they could focus-group it. Lulu doesn't want to spend

---

**10 awesome things negotiating can get you**

Lower rent

A higher allowance

Two for the price of one

Free shipping

A backrub (in my case, in exchange for doing laundry)

Store credit

The release of at least one hostage

A baked potato instead of fries, at no extra charge

A second VIP pass for your friend

Five more minutes

---

millions on a product line that nobody likes or can do yoga in without looking like an idiot, so yeah, maybe do some market research.

(Also: use some common sense.)

**Death by focus group (DBFG)** happens when a smaller, not-very-diverse group of people get together to analyze something they actually have a stake in — such as a new company logo, rules for the condominium association, or where you should have your mom's surprise seventieth-birthday party.

In these situations, and just like the random customers surveyed by Lululemon, the focus group participants each have their own valid opinions. But those opinions get complicated by one or more of the following:

- Worrying about contradicting boss/coworkers

- Avoiding conflict

- Being the wrong demographic for the product/idea

- Actually caring one way or another, i.e., having an agenda

- Other miscellaneous baggage

At the end of *this* kind of informal focus group process, you typically end up with a "safe" result, in the sense that **nobody hates it but nobody really loves it.** *Everyone* knows there's something that could be better, but no one has the courage or conviction to take a stand.

That is, unless somebody decides to get difficult.

Unfortunately, you can't always escape the focus group, but at least you can breathe a little life into it — and simultaneously save everyone else from themselves. For example:

- At work, don't be afraid to make your voice heard when the group-approved logo looks like something your cat did in Photoshop.

- Among neighbors, don't let a bunch of Lazy Larrys keep the whole building from staying up to code.

- And if you're Skyping with your siblings to plan your mom's party, don't be afraid to say, "Who needs another 'festive brunch' with mini-cupcakes and endive salad? Our mother deserves a trip to Vegas to see *Magic Mike Live,* and if you're not willing to make it happen, I'll book two tickets for her and me, and we'll just see whose name figures prominently in the will."

This crusade against DBFG may seem frivolous—especially when other gurus are out there curing cancer with plastic charm bracelets or whatever—but I have a clear objective in bolstering your defenses against this very real and present threat. Because mark my words: **When the Zombie Apocalypse comes, focus group mentality will be the literal death of us all.**

# A taste test

Have you ever cried at work? I already told you about that time I cried in the town house when my boss yelled at me, but that was by no means the peak of my crying-at-work *oeuvre*. Oh, how I have wept in cubicles! I've sniffled and snuffled in ladies' rooms. I've fought back tears in the doorway of many a boss, only to shed them, copiously, in the privacy of my own hard-won office.

A memorable sob session occurred a few years ago when my then-boss told me I had "difficult" taste.

Some context: For more than a decade, my job as an acquiring editor for major publishing houses was to discover writers and stories that were worth sharing and that were ALSO capable of finding a large enough audience to make money on behalf of the company. Something like a million books are published each year in the US alone, and I was responsible for finding and nurturing about ten of them. I enjoyed a more-than-respectable career in terms of sales and review coverage for my books — they were nominated for awards, optioned for film, and sold in dozens of countries.

But did they all make a profit? Hell no. THEY RARELY DO, SON.

The harsh reality is that most books fail. They fail to find a large enough audience. They fail to win acclaim or sometimes even passing mention. They fail to make money. It's just the way the business works (or doesn't work, as the case may be), and it's something every editor knows and grapples with, year in and year out. We, and our peers in the sales and publicity and marketing departments, confront failure every day.

To top it off, most publishers are susceptible to the

mind-set that "if X worked, then all books like X will always work," and "if Y didn't work, than nothing like Y will ever work." So as soon as you go to market with one thing that doesn't sell like you'd hoped, suddenly all of the similar stuff you have on the docket is subject to fatal second-guesswork.

(One time, the CEO of a major house declined to let me bid aggressively enough to win a future multimillion-copy bestseller because "Cat books don't work." Who wishes they'd been a little more open-minded meow?)

Anyway, in this particular conversation I had a few years ago with this particular boss, he reasoned that the books I gravitated toward—often about dark subjects like sexual violence or drug abuse, or featuring unsympathetic narrators—were too "difficult" to sell, and that I might want to change my approach to what I liked, in order to make life "easier" on myself and the colleagues charged with publicizing and marketing the stuff I brought in.

Well.

I'm a real pain in the ass, but I can take constructive criticism. (Eventually. Usually after I stew about it for half an hour.) What burned my biscuits about this little tête-à-tête was not my boss's assessment of my taste. He wasn't wrong that the books I liked most were harder to sell than, say, books about old white people, to old white people. Old white people are very easy targets.*

Nor was he being especially critical or threatening about it, just maddeningly matter-of-fact.

What made me go back to my office and cry was the implication that it was pointless to even try to stay true to myself. That, in one of the most creative industries in the world, I shouldn't stray *too* far out of the box. That I should turn my back on what I liked and open my arms to whatever came easy.

Successful publishing boils down to finding and connecting with an audience. So it seemed to me that blaming the kinds of books that I liked and understood for the difficulties of the business as a whole was somewhat misguided. I mean, yes, we all have to worry about the bottom line — but was the solution really to cut out an entire audience altogether?

---

* My boss did not use the words "old white people." I am extrapolating based on fifteen years in the industry and a hundred such conversations.

"Sorry, folks who like to read about dark, sinister, salacious, controversial subjects. You'll have to spend your money somewhere else. We don't serve your kind here."

As you might imagine, the idea of sticking to "easier" subjects and "friendlier" voices that were "more palatable to the masses" made me die a little inside. After I self-administered some Visine and half a Xanax behind my closed office door, I decided I wasn't willing to accept "difficult" for an answer. I knew there had to be enough people like me out there to do business with, so I dug in my heels and fought harder and smarter to find and connect with them.

In that way, my boss's decree of difficulty was helpful. **It lit a fire of *Fuck it* under me, to prove that I didn't have to commit focus group seppuku to succeed.**

I'm happy to say that after I left that job, three of the "difficult" projects I'd left behind became bestsellers, which is a good stat for our business. (It would be like batting .333 in the majors, so, better than Joe DiMaggio, but not quite Shoeless Joe.) I'm not saying those sales were my doing — I'm just the proud middlewoman between great books and satisfied readers. But ultimately my affinity for unsympathetic narrators and dark, twisted, gritty, and taboo subjects did connect with a big audience AND make oodles of money for my former company — which was always the objective — and I didn't have to compromise my taste to get it done.

Being difficult, for the win!

(Oh, and to my delight, I also had a second chance to publish a bestselling cat book. *Felines of New York*. Check it out.)

---

### Use your powers for good, not evil

If you're like me and don't often take the easy way in, then you also rarely get caught taking the easy way *out*. That's good. Keep it up! We stand up for what we believe in — yes, potentially making our own and other people's lives more difficult in the process — but we won't turn tail and run when the going gets tough, either. Our friends can count on us to avenge their honor online; our families can count on us to complain to the front desk so they don't have to; and our fellow citizens can count on us to write scathingly accurate TripAdvisor reviews and donate regularly to Amnesty International. When push comes to shove, everyone's better off with a difficult person in their corner.

---

# God, why do you have to be so *difficult?*

I already told you: because it usually works out better for me. But you know what? Sometimes it's difficult to be so difficult! Mostly because other people don't appreciate all the good you're doing for them. I do it anyway, because I think that **when the going gets tough, having the courage of your convictions is admirable** — especially when you have, like, sixteen better things to be doing than defending your needs, desires, and values to a bunch of people who don't understand why you care so deeply about anything they do not care deeply about.

In that case, all you have to do is *understand* that they are impoverished by their own narrow-mindedness, and keep on doing your thing.

BOOM.

# Do Be a Team Player*

## *On the contrary, you can do YOU all by yourself.

I'm not too proud to admit that I remember my high school yearbook quote without having to look it up, or that twenty years later, it's still right *on fucking target:**

> I would rather sit on a pumpkin and have it all to myself, than be crowded on a velvet cushion.
> — Henry David Thoreau

Yes, I was a precocious little shit who read *Walden* while other kids my age attended pep rallies and polished off the Babysitters Club franchise. (And there is nothing

---

\* I am, however, too proud to admit that I still know where my high school yearbook is.

wrong with any of those pursuits. You do you, Wells High Class of '96!) But my young love affair with transcendentalism served me well later in life, so that pumpkin is where this story begins.

(Okay, technically it begins on a tree stump. Specifically: the neatly felled remnant of an old oak that sat on the front right corner of our yard in Maine.)

Many twilight hours in my single-digit youth were occupied by sitting on my stump. I perched there to read, to daydream, and to rehearse a debate with my parents over dropping the "h" from the end of my name.*

And when the neighbor kid's mother caught us playing doctor (for the second time) and told me to go think about what I'd done, well, I headed straight for my stump. Did I mention it was located on a hill overlooking the neighbors' garden and front steps? In retrospect, it was probably slightly creepy for me to sit there as often as I did, contemplating the universe fifty feet from their bay window.

---

* "It's so obtrusive!" I argued, when really I just thought "Sara" was more of a cute-girl name than "Sarah." Told you I was a precocious little shit.

Look, as I believe I have already made abundantly clear: NOBODY'S PERFECT.

Anyway, for as long as I can remember, I've spent a lot of time alone. I do a fair bit of thinking, mulling, and pondering, which requires peace and quiet. I'm a big reader, which is hard to do with people around — they're always interrupting with their "need for human interaction" and their "What do you want for dinner, sweetheart?" (Hi, babe. Love you!)

Also, I can rarely be bothered to wear pants, which makes me awkward company.

But the thing is, I also really *like* being by myself. I like working on my own so I don't have to run things by other people. It serves both my ego and my zeal for efficiency, and it's why I write books with a single byline, instead of TV shows. Vying for the chance to share an Emmy fifteen ways would turn me into the Mommie Dearest of any Hollywood writers' room. (*I. SAID. NO. FART. JOKES. WHAT ARE FART JOKES DOING IN THIS SCEEEEEEENE?!?*) And although my husband is an accomplished cook, sometimes I just want to dismantle a large cheese pizza, on my own, with my hands — and without pausing to compliment the chef.

You can see how spending a few hours a week sitting

on a stump was the perfect activity for a kid who'd rather collect her thoughts than invitations to sleepovers. (Though let's be honest, it's not like I was swimming in those, either.) Nobody even *wants* to sit down next to you on a stump. There's not much room, for one. It's also not terribly comfortable, and then there's the lichen to consider; that stuff can really mark up your shorts.

But I'll tell you what — if I had a stump today, I'd absolutely ride that puppy for an hour to avoid a board meeting, a baby shower, or anything described on the invite as a "mixer." Actually, you know, I guess I sort of do have one, but it's in my pool, it's called "an inflatable pineapple," and it is a big improvement. (Sorry, Stumpy.)

Where was I?

Oh, right, so in my yearbook quote from *Walden*, Thoreau was not professing his love for solitude, but I think seventeen-year-olds can be forgiven for seeing what they want to see. Rather, he was expressing his preference for a simple life, uncluttered by the trappings of wealth and consumer culture. Just before the pumpkin bit, he writes:

> I had three pieces of limestone on my desk, but I was terrified to find that they required to be dusted

daily, when the furniture of my mind was all undusted still, and threw them out the window in disgust. How, then, could I have a furnished house? I would rather sit in the open air, for no dust gathers on the grass, unless where man has broken ground.

Okay, whoa, I just realized that Thoreau was the original decluttering guru. The ODG! And "the furniture of my mind"??? Shit, he got to mental redecorating before me, too. I knew I liked that guy.

With his wisdom in mind, I'd like to spend a little more time extolling **the pleasures of the DIY life, both in terms of being alone, and of making (and being solely responsible for) your own decisions.**

As my grandfather used to say, "It's nice work if you can get it."

# One is the loveliest number

Lately I feel like I've been seeing a lot of articles about "extroverted introverts" — people who do go out to parties, but they stick toward the edges of the room, lose their verve quickly, and would otherwise describe themselves as shy. And perhaps a touch reclusive.

This section is for them, as well as for people more like me, whom I would call **"antisocial socials."**

See, I happen to be quite good at socializing, and when I'm into it, hoo boy, I'm up there dancing on the bar with a coconut on my head. I have an entire Facebook album called "Stuff on My Head" devoted to this pursuit. (And no, I will not accept your friend request just so you can see it. Do I know you?)

However, I'm just as often *not* into it — not because I'm shy or have social anxiety, but because **I don't particularly like most people, and forced interaction is my idea of a war crime.**

I see some of you nodding along, so I want to emphasize that **it's not weird or bad to prefer the company of yourself over others.** You're not alone in

### God bless theater people

Of course every rule has its exception, and in the case of "People, Not Liking Most of —," mine would be *theater* people. Marching to the beat of their own Flower Drum Song, the folks I've had the pleasure of serving with in casts and on crews over the years have been high-quality, low-maintenance, hardworking, softhearted, and even more fun than Bette Midler in a bathhouse.

wanting to be alone. (I would say that we loners need to stick together, but obviously that would be both unpleasant and unsanitary.)

For people like us, sitting by ourselves on a stump or a couch for three hours can be just as pleasant and invigorating as taking a group walking tour of the Parthenon can be for others.* A chance to clear our minds, let down our guards, and reconnect with ourselves. Or just take off our bras and let the girls roam free for an afternoon. Bliss.

Whether you identify as an introvert, an extroverted introvert, or an antisocial social, **protecting your solitude is paramount to living a happy life.** You may have to say "No thank you" or "I can't make it" on the occasional (or more-than-occasional) basis. Is that selfish? Sure, but it's solidly in the Self-Care Zone. And even the most social animals among us could still use a breather. I once read that if given the chance, a puppy will continue playing with a rotating cast of humans with no breaks and no sleep until it *dies*.

Don't be that puppy.

———

* Hello, and WELCOME TO MY PERSONAL HELL.

**Even if you think of yourself as a very social person, being alone has undeniable benefits**. Here are half a dozen off the top of my head:

---

### 6 benefits of being alone

1. There are fewer dishes to wash after lunch.
2. Especially if you took this opportunity to eat something out of a takeout container using your finger as a fork.
3. Nobody is here to judge you for listening to *The Best of UB40: Volumes I and II*, nonstop, in their entirety.
4. You can get through a whole episode of *Game of Thrones* without anyone asking you why Jaime Lannister puts up with Cersei's bullshit.
5. You're free to pass gas with impunity.
6. Three words: no tan lines.

---

Enticing, no?

Take it from me: You can enjoy the company of your friends but still choose a day to yourself over a lovely invitation to a ball game or a barbecue. You can love being with your partner yet still cherish your alone time. (My husband is my favorite person, but he is not infrequently instructed to please go away now.)

Unfortunately some of your friends and loved ones

may not understand your yen for "you time," and when you try to beg off or bow out, they don't take the hint. *But it's such a beautiful day! Come on, if you join us we can get the group rate!* They're not being jerks, they just really like you and want to hang out as much as possible, at 10 percent off.

That's nice…for them.

If you continue to demur, they may even feel slighted. They're entitled. **But you're entitled to put preserving your own sanity ahead of assuaging other people's egos or filling out their urban scavenger hunt team.**

Ultimately—and for everyone involved—it's much better to declare what you want, need, and deserve up front than to get pushed to the point of "FOR THE LOVE OF GOD GET OUT OF MY FACE BEFORE I *END* YOU."

If you don't believe me, just ask my husband.

# There's no "o" in "team," either. What's your point?

Some of my best friends are team players. It's not a bad way to go through life—it's just that NOT being one gets more than its fair share of criticism, even though plenty of us simply were not built for team sports, team-building exercises, and team pub trivia (a topic on which I made my feelings known in the original no-fucks-given guide).

Personally, I prefer playing with myself.

Ahem.

My issue with teams is that **as often as they may achieve a common goal, they can also take advantage of individuals.** And when you're the individual who's dragging the whole team down, it can be traumatizing.

For example, being forced to play volleyball during gym class may have been good for my cardiovascular health, but it wasn't exactly kind to my self-esteem. Plus, if I played the only way I knew how — stand quietly at the back of the court and cover my eyes — I put my team-mates' win in jeopardy. I felt bad about that. What did Mr. McLeod have against "Who wants to sit on this nice sturdy bench over here and keep score? Sarah? Great, here's a pencil."

If this sounds like you, you don't have to wait around to get put on the roster. Try *volunteering* to be Official Scorekeeper right up front. In gym class or in life, if you can come up with a reasonable way to contribute to the greater good while staying out of the scrum, why not? You'll be happier, safer, and less sweaty, and the peeps who are really into serving, setting, and spiking can have all the "fun."

**Other times, you might be the individual who's getting trampled by everyone else.**

I don't know about you, but my teachers were always urging me to "cooperate," a skill they seemed to revere alongside addition, subtraction, spelling, and raising your hand to go to the bathroom. Yet when I was forced into working on a group project, it usually meant me doing 90 percent of it and the other three kids taking turns raising their hands to go to the bathroom — or in the case of one early-adopting fifth grader I knew, sneaking out to smoke a cigarette in the stairwell.

Not cool, Kristi.

This trend continued in my adult life, with employers asking me to "take one for the team" and "play well with others" *even while admitting that the "others" in question were not pulling their weight.* No wonder I hate company picnics, which combine the worst of both gym class and the workplace in one endless afternoon of trust falls and soggy pasta salad.

(Remember those WNDs from page 33? I identified the fuck out of "I want to make my own decisions" and held it close when I quit my corporate job to work for myself.)

So what does this deep dive into my antisocial, uncoordinated, uncooperative past have to do with you? Well, if you didn't decide to skip this chapter when you read the title, then I'm guessing you and I are two of a kind—peas in a pod, except both of us would rather have the pod to ourselves. I'll further wager that if you bought the book in the first place, you could use a little help asserting your individuality. Fair to say?

Well, sometimes the best way to escape Lowest Common Denominator Living is to remove the "common" part altogether and **do it your way from the get-go.** Lucky for you, I am now a certified expert in doing things my way. Here's how it works:

**First, you have to stop giving a fuck about what other people think.** I went into great detail on this in my first book, and for the sake of readers who've already mastered NGAF and the NotSorry Method, I don't want to repeat myself too much, but essentially this entails worrying only about what you can control (your own behavior) and not about what you can't (other people's opinions).

Go ahead and record stats from the sidelines or install yourself rigid and unmoving at backcourt like it's fucking Easter Island. Your teammates will get over it. Don't spend your time and energy worrying about what people will think about you "doing it your way."

**Just do it.**

(The key is not to be an asshole *while* doing it. I gave a twelve-minute TEDx talk on this. Treat yo'self.)*

**Finally, be prepared to take responsibility.** It's not unreasonable to trust your instincts and/or work ethic over someone else's. A healthy distrust of your fellow man's ability to get the quarterly numbers in on time could save you a lot of heartache during audit season. But — and I know this may come as a surprise — your way will not *always* be the correct or most successful one.

Here at You Do You HQ, we don't claim to necessarily be the best and brightest, and we recognize the fact that every special snowflake has as many distinctive ways to mess shit up as they do to get it right.

If you find yourself on the ass-end of one of your less triumphant solo maneuvers, it's important to [wo]man up

---

* www.youtube.com/watch?v=GwRzjFQa_Og

and learn from it. Your way is an acceptable route, but backing yourself into a small, petty, delusional corner is no one's idea of a fun detour.

Hey, come for the flowcharts, stay for the real talk.

Next up: the final "don't" of Part II, and one with which I am intimately familiar...

# Don't Quit Your Day Job<sup>*</sup>

*Take risks, ignore the doubters, and
prove the haters wrong.*

Fun fact: You wouldn't be reading this persuasive ode to
personal empowerment if I had not actually quit my
actual day job a couple of years ago. I know — so meta you
can hardly stand it, right? Samesies. But it's true, and it's a
positively textbook example of the knowledge I'm about
to drop.

However, the story behind that Big Life Decision is
one I've already told twice in two books, focusing first on
*why* I quit (to give fewer, better fucks) and second on *how* I
quit (by getting my shit together). So if you want to read
about those aspects of my "personal journey" — and yes, I
just threw up in my mouth as I typed those words — you
know where to find 'em.

What I'm exploring here is a little different. I want to

talk about **taking risks,** whether or not they are specifically related to your employment situation.

Sure, you might hear "Don't quit your day job" when you tell people you're ditching your nine-to-five gig, pouring your meager savings into Mime College, and moving to Paris with only a beret and a dream (though you will emphatically NOT hear it from any mimes). But even if spooning with your employer-matched pension keeps you sleeping peacefully at night, someday you're liable to catch those five little words thrown at you, under different circumstances, by someone who feels the need to knock you down a peg.

Whatever the case — if you're contemplating a big audition, a big purchase, or a big haircut — when Judgy McJudgerson sneers, scoffs, or jokes "Don't quit your day job," he's really saying, **"That sounds risky. I wouldn't."** Perhaps with a subtle note of **"I don't believe in you, so you probably shouldn't believe in you either."** (Or just "I don't believe you have the cheekbones to pull that off.")

Why Judgy gotta be like that?

Well, I'm going to hold back my slappin' hand for a sec and give everyone's favorite killjoy a smidge of leeway on this topic. Because although making snarky comments about other people's life choices is frowned upon, **the social contract is heavy on maintaining a shared sense of security**—so if YOU start fucking around with norms and going off the grid of safe, sensible, conservative decision-making, where does that leave Judgy?

Afraid, that's where.

And fear is a BITCH. (More on that later...)

Of course, watching people take risks can be exhilarating. Especially if it's from the comfort and safety of your couch, as when I watched tightrope artist Nik Wallenda walk live over the Grand Canyon. He had a 6,000-foot-deep yawning chasm; I had a box of White Cheddar Cheez-Its. Exciting stuff. But sometimes—or at the same time—bearing witness to risk can be scary and unsettling. It begs one to imagine being in the other person's shoes (in the case of Nik Wallenda, handmade, ankle-height, elkskin shoes), and one (like our pal Judgy) reacts by not only taking a big step away from the rim of the rock formation, but trying to drag you back with him.

So yeah, Judgy's got some shit to deal with, and I don't envy him for it. But *just because* he doesn't like being too close to the edge doesn't mean it's no place for a nice girl like you to hang out.

And hey, risks aren't just for Flying Wallendas — I have plenty of friends who look stable on résumés and bank statements but, on weekends, can be found with their head in a shark's mouth or taking fire-eating classes. Even naturally risk-averse people like yours truly who stay the hell away from motorcycles and hot air balloons will someday be tempted by the road less traveled.

**Taking it doesn't have to be as scary as Judgy (or you) might think.**

# Risky business

*You Do You* is as much a self-help book as it is a postmortem on my own midlife renaissance,* which has involved taking a few big risks in the last few years.

---

* The life expectancy for American women is currently 79.13 years, so as of this writing, I couldn't be more midlife if I *tried*.

In addition to exiting the rat race, starting my own business, and convincing a publisher I was capable of writing not one but three postmortems on my midlife renaissance disguised as self-help books, in 2016 my husband and I uprooted our entire life to move from Brooklyn, New York, to a tiny fishing village in the Dominican Republic.

And if you had told sixteen- or twenty-six-year-old me that thirty-six-year-old me would jettison not only a thriving career but also a lovely apartment and a stable, comfortable existence for a complete 180-degree turn toward a life of unknowns, adventure, and snakes in her roof* — she would have lobbied to have thirty-six-year-old me preemptively committed.

All of this is to say, I know a little something about risk, so if you feel like you're ready to ditch your real or metaphorical day job, and if you're looking for a wee push off of the cliff, it would be my pleasure to provide one. Metaphorically.

---

* "*On* her roof?" asked her editor. "No, definitely *in* her roof," she answered. "Jesus fucking Christ," he replied.

## 5 types of risks you could take and how to approach them

**Changing your look:** Shaving your head, getting a tattoo, going Goth, or just going blond — a makeover can be subtle or bold, and none of it has to be forever. Hair grows back, wardrobes can be retrofitted, and lasers are very sophisticated these days. So why not experiment? These are the best kinds of risks to take — fun and semipermanent. Barely counts at all, frankly. **Risk level: Get thee to a tattoo parlor!**

**Auditioning for something**: Whether it's community theater or an internationally syndicated talent competition, the worst thing that can happen — after strutting your stuff under the watchful eye of Post Office Joan (who's directing this year's outer space–set *Sweeney Todd*) or warbling before your secret man crush Adam Levine — is that Joan or Adam tells you "Sorry, it's a no from me." So go polish up that monologue, get your octaves in order, and give it a shot. **Risk level: Deep breaths.**

**Making a big purchase**: If you have a bunch of bank in the tank, then buying a house or a car isn't necessarily a risk; it's just a thing you do every five to ten years. Congratulations, that's a nice way to be able to go through life! But for most of us, deciding to use our limited resources to buy a big-ticket item or pay for grad school is more than a little daunting. These are upward-mobility risks. They could improve your life more, even, than a star turn in outer space–set *Sweeney Todd*, but the upfront cost is a lot greater than a case of the jitters. True, the scariest thing I ever did was sign my name to a mortgage, but I steeled my nerves with math. Figure out what you can afford, either in a lump sum or monthly loan payments, and don't overextend yourself. **Risk level: Calculated.**

**Wearing your heart on your sleeve**: Are you itching to say those three little words? Maybe gearing up to get down on one knee? Or just hoping your cute study buddy will check the "Yes" box next to "Do you *like me* like me?" with a big, fat flourish? It may seem like a big deal in the moment, but look at it this way: In each case, the outcome is binary. I know, SUPER-ROMANTIC, SARAH. But she either loves you back, or she doesn't. He'll either say yes, or he won't. One box will get checked and the other will remain as cold and empty as your bed on a winter's night. Whatevs. The potential for heartache is real, but doing nothing just so you can't possibly be disappointed is its own form of self-torture. Who are you, the Marquis de Sade? **Risk level: Zeroes and ones.**

**Starting a side hustle:** Totally intimidating, no arguments there. Booting up a new business — whether it's web design or an Etsy store — can bring great reward or complete and utter failure, plus, potentially, a lot of useless candle-making equipment in your apartment. The key to getting anything like this up and running is a combination of strategy, focus, and commitment. I go over all of that stuff in *Get Your Shit Together,* but it comes AFTER you decide to start the business. In terms of taking the risk in the first place, I can tell you that *fortuna audaces iuvat.* That's a Latin proverb that means it takes balls to make money. **Risk level: Grow a pair.**

And once you decide to take a risk (Bravo! I knew you had it in ya!), how do you keep walking the walk while other people are talking the shit-talk?

## Top 3 ways to silence the haters

**Fly under the radar:** When my husband and I were planning our move to the DR, we told virtually no one. Why? Because we didn't want to have to field questions, explain ourselves, or entertain naysayers. What other people don't know won't hurt them, *and* you won't have to talk about it at brunch.

**Screen your calls:** If it's not feasible to hide your risk under a bushel, you can limit your exposure to negative energy the same way I limit my exposure to street vendors, phishing scams, and telemarketers — don't engage. If someone wants to pooh-pooh your life choices in person, make an excuse and walk away. ("Sorry, I'm late!" is a good one.) If they email you, don't respond. And if they call you up, just "accidentally" switch off your ringer. Oops.

**Clap back:** If you're feeling sassy, just say, "Thanks but no thanks for your unsolicited opinion. I'll be sure to return the favor someday when you are on the verge of making a well-thought-out, nerve-wracking decision that you were nonetheless quite confident in before I opened my yap."

Ultimately, if other people doubt your potential for greatness, that's one thing. Other people can be kept in the dark, ignored, and put in their place.

But what do you do when the voices are coming from inside your own head?

# I wish I knew how to quit you*

At fifteen years old, I tried to quit my summer job at a local surf and turf restaurant. I was really unhappy for a lot of reasons and it was the tail end of the season. I

---

* A longer version of this anecdote appeared on Medium in 2015, in an essay called "I Quit My Job Today (And so can you!)." I repurposed some of it here because it's EXTRA-RELEVANT to this chapter.

thought I could quit and at least enjoy my Labor Day weekend, far from buckets of dirty mop water and the scallop-scented fry batter that clung like barnacles to my Gap slacks.

I rehearsed my quitting speech only slightly fewer times than I rehearsed that TEDx talk I mentioned earlier, then mustered my *cojones* and went into the owner's office to ask him to take me off the schedule.

Permanently.

When the four-minute conversation was over I was near tears and shaking with what I now recognize as panic but at the time felt like imminent death. To add insult to injury, my mother was waiting in the parking lot to pick me up from my shift. Heaving my *cojones* wordlessly into her minivan, I couldn't bring myself to tell her right away what I'd done.

Somehow I instinctively felt as if quitting had been wrong, even though my reasons felt absolutely right.

The next morning, my boss called to inform my parents of my "rash" decision and asked them to intervene, saying I was too important to the successful operation of the restaurant to lose at this critical juncture. (Let me be clear: This is like saying that a single fifteen-year-old in the Zhengzhou factory is critical to Apple making its quarterly numbers.)

My boss knew that my presence or absence was not likely to alter the fate of his glorified-Applebee's establishment during the dog days of August, but he also knew he could ruin the paltry remains of my summer by pulling "parent rank." And given my anxiety-laced speech the night before, he probably also suspected that he'd be outing me before I'd had a chance to let Mom and Dad know I was not the future valedictorian they thought they'd raised, but rather a sniveling little quitter.

True, I wasn't leaving for a better gig or more money. I wasn't building a career in food service that necessitated a move up the ladder to Mike's Clam Shack, nor had I been diagnosed with a severe shellfish allergy. (I also wasn't feeding my family on my $2.30 an hour—it was just a summer job.) I simply wasn't happy, and I didn't want to show up. Another. Single. Fucking. Day.

But of course I went back, apron strings between my legs. Guilt and shame can be powerful motivators. Quitters never win, and all that.

## Actually, sometimes when people quit, we all win

Imagine, for a moment, that Barack Obama had decided not to quit his day job as a US senator to assume the presidency in 2009. At the last minute, he was like, "Nah, guys, never mind, I'm going to stick with what I know." Or if Meat Loaf had decided not to blow off his gig as a nightclub bouncer to audition for the Los Angeles production of *Hair*, which led to him meeting his longtime collaborator, Jim Steinman.

The world would be a much bleaker place, would it not?

People who exit their comfort zones and parachute into the Great Unknown have long been rewarded for their guts and mettle — and they've given the rest of us eight years of global dignity and the perennial pleasure of "Paradise by the Dashboard Light." Thanks, Obama. Thanks, Loaf.

Anyway, that whole incident set off a little audio loop in my brain that went something like: *Quitting is a bad thing. It's a personal failure. It's not only a cultural no-no, but a rejection of the masochistic Puritan work ethic this country was built on, goddammit.*

That voice piped up quite a few more times over the next twenty years, like when I worked at a bookstore where I was routinely derided by my manager, Wendy-

Ann, for "being a know-it-all" (also known as "having read the books I was recommending to the customers"). But I had signed on during the fall rush—students at the nearby college bought their textbooks from this shop—so I kept my commitment even when I got a career-track offer to work for a prestigious literary agent. I pulled sixteen-hour weekends at the store while starting my new gig as an agent's assistant during the week.

Wouldn't want Wendy-Ann to think I was a know-it-all *and* a welcher.

Nearly a year into the agent's assistant job, I was developing secondhand emphysema from being confined to an office all day with a two-pack-a-day smoker who also turned out to be verbally abusive, pickled in Chardonnay, and very, very cheap. Did I want to quit suddenly and spectacularly with no safety net? Almost every day. But did I responsibly seek out new employment and then magnanimously offer my soon-to-be-ex-boss a full month's notice — *during the holidays* — before leaving? Yes to that, too.

(And still, when I showed up a couple of months later to pay my respects at her mother's wake, she introduced me to the gathered crowd as "the assistant who abandoned me when my mother was dying," ensuring that even after doing everything aboveboard, I now felt retroactively bad about quitting.)

After that, I held a series of jobs in publishing that I only quit for the sake of a raise, a promotion, or upward mobility in the form of slightly less jankity office furniture and a company BlackBerry. This kind of quitting seemed — per the social contract — to be the only acceptable way to do it.

That's how I operated until two years ago, when I quit my most recent day job for the same reasons that I tried to walk out of the Bull & Claw in the summer of 1995. I didn't have a better offer. I hadn't won the lottery. I simply wanted to be HAPPIER, and the only way to accomplish that was:

1. **Face my fear of being judged, criticized, and looked down upon for being "a quitter."**

2. **Step off the motherfucking ledge.**

For some people, step 2 might be the hardest. For me, the risks of leaving behind a salary and benefits and facing the challenges of starting my own freelance business were daunting, but I had plans to account for them. (In case you don't know this about me: I'm big on plans.)

It was step 1 that had been keeping me up at night. I could hear Judgy, firing a warning shot across my pillow.

*If you do this and it doesn't work out, they'll never take you back, you know. You'll have proven you didn't deserve your day job to begin with, and* then *where will you be? This sounds risky. I wouldn't. Oh and PS, I don't believe in you, so you probably shouldn't believe in you either. PPS Now is probably NOT the time for a drastic haircut.*

Fast-forward a couple of years and I think I can safely say quitting was the right choice for me. (I can also nominate that last sentence for Understatement of the Millennium.) And at some point while I was falling asleep for the first time in a long time without dreading my morning commute, I realized it hadn't been Judgy whispering sweet nothings in my ear after all.

Much as I'd like to — and a bit of a theme in this chapter — I can't blame him for this one.

# Midnight in the garden of obligation, guilt, and fear

When it comes to taking risks, **the seed of doubt can often be found growing out of YOUR VERY OWN BRAIN**. It was planted there by a culture that values stability, and it thrives on obligation, guilt, and fear.

Much like marigolds get planted in real gardens to keep insects away from the more useful stuff (at least, that's what I think marigolds are for), doubt is there for a reason—to preserve stability—which is often a very good thing, in work, finances, relationships, and the like.

You just can't give the marigolds of doubt *unlimited access* **to obligation, guilt, and fear,** or they take over the whole joint.

It's absolutely fine to tend the seeds. Acknowledge their purpose. Let them know that you know that they know that you know they're there, and let them blossom just enough to do their job, but not so they smother everything in the vicinity.

Here are three questions you can ask yourself to keep the marigolds of doubt in check:

**• Do you have an OBLIGATION to anyone else that factors into that risk you've been mulling?**

You might think, *Yes, yes I do!* But is it a true obligation — like to people who depend on you financially? Legitimate obligations are beneficial weeds, like oh, I don't know, pennycress or clover.* Those are there to help you balance out your whole garden. Doesn't mean you can't yank them at some point, just don't be too hasty. However, if it's an imagined obligation — like, that people might be disappointed in your choice even though it doesn't affect them at all — then it's just a regular weed, like crabgrass. Yank away.

**• Do you feel GUILTY about whatever risk you're about to take?**

Perhaps you want to run for president of your sorority even though your best friend has already declared

---

* Of course I looked up "beneficial weeds" to make this analogy. The only beneficial weed I know anything about isn't legal everywhere books are sold.

her candidacy. That might get messy, and you're not wrong to feel a little conflicted. But if it's important to you and you're not doing it just to spite her, you don't have anything to feel guilty about. On the other hand, if you're about to risk a friendship over something stupid—like shagging your buddy's ex and hoping he doesn't find out about it—stand down, Casanova. Some guilt is called for and some isn't. Just be vigilant, or it will eat up ALL of your plants like a green hornworm caterpillar. Have you Google-imaged one of those lately? (Don't.)

**• Do you FEAR what might happen after you take that risk?**

Some fear is healthy—like, eating poison blowfish and barebacking may not be the risks you want to stake your crop on. (Far be it from me to judge, but in cases like these I'd say the marigolds of doubt are doing their job; fear is keeping them suitably vibrant.) Again though, it's all about balance. If you sow constant, unrelenting fear in your mind-garden, you might as well drop a big blue tarp over the whole thing and let the weeds and caterpillars duke it out for supremacy. My money's on the caterpillars.

## *BONUS QUESTION*

• **Do you FEAR being judged and criticized just for considering this risk in the first place?**

Ah, and just like that, we've come full circle. Fear: IT'S A BITCH. You'll remember that the biggest fear I had when I was weighing the risks of quitting my day job was "what other people would think," and that fear — a big blue tarp decades in the weaving — kept me, for a very long time, from making what turned out to be one of the best decisions of my LIFE.

**In the end, my only regret wasn't over the risk I took, but the fact that I didn't take it sooner.** (But that quote sounds like it belongs on another cheesy motivational poster, superimposed over a photo of Eleanor Roosevelt or, like, Mark Twain's mustache, and we can't have that, people. I've got standards to maintain.)

YOU MIGHT DIE TOMORROW. TAKE A RISK TODAY.

It's like I said at the beginning of this chapter: "Don't quit your day job" is a stand-in for all kinds of reasons not to take all kinds of risks. And whether it's running for office, getting a perm, or moving to a foreign country famous for its jungle fauna, don't let anybody — be it Judgy McJudgerson or your own irrational brain — tell you that you CAN'T take it.

Or for that matter, that you WON'T succeed, it WON'T look good, or you WILL regret it.

Coincidentally, this brings us to Part III. Funny how that works.

||

# WILLs & WON'Ts:
Not-so-great expectations

Don't you love it when your friends and family — or total strangers — go all Miss Cleo and tell you what's bound to happen as a result of *your* life choices? These people should be playing the stock market, they're so talented at predicting futures!

**Part III deals with expectations — other people's, that is — and how they don't have to affect you, if you don't let them.**

For the record, I think it's important to manage expectations — to let someone, be it a boss, coworker, friend, or partner, know what they're going to get from you before you give it. This way, nobody has reason to be disappointed when you deliver exactly what you promised. **I do not, however, like to be ruled by expectations anyone else sets *for* me.** I prefer to set the goalposts — and if I erect them outside the bounds of what "normal" people do with their "conventional" lives, I don't need play-by-play commentary from the sidelines.

Especially in the form of **"You will change your mind."** Hence the introductory chapter of Part III, on making unconventional life choices that inexplicably bother other people who don't have to live them.

Beyond being told what choices I will or won't be

making, another thing that aggravates me is **being told how I will or won't feel *after* I make those choices.** Really? Are you hooked into my brain like the Matrix or some shit? Listen, I've had more regrets about forgetting to eat leftover Indian food before it went bad than many people have about filing for divorce, and conversely, I still don't regret never having finished *Breaking Bad*. Simmer down, Morpheus. You don't know my life.

In the chapter called **"You will regret that,"** we'll go over the difference between right, wrong, and what other people *tell you* is wrong, and how to avoid getting suckered into "preemptive regret." Not that there isn't room for responsible info-gathering **if you want or need others' feedback in order to make a decision** — but Part III isn't about entertaining your friend Claire's helpful advice on switching cell phone providers. It's about not allowing your desires, feelings, hopes, or regrets to be described for you in detail — before they occur — by someone else who has no fucking idea what they're talking about.

The fact is: Nobody (you included) is in possession of a functioning crystal ball, so nobody (me included) can really tell you what will transpire if you make certain choices. **Letting other people's *expectations* get in the** way of your *experience*—and of learning from it—is no way to live.

But wait, there's more!

In **"You won't get anywhere with that attitude,"** a paean to pessimism, I'll present the merits of being a glass-half-empty kinda gal. In **"You won't get a good job if you don't go to college,"** we'll look at different versions of success, and I'll explain why you and only you can decide what you make of any of them. And in **"You will never live that down"**—a chapter devoted to the art of being weird—we're gonna run that freak flag up the pole and let it fly.

My advice? Keep reading. You won't regret it.

# You Will Change
# Your Mind*

*About unconventional lifestyle choices
that inexplicably bother people who
don't have to live them? Probably not.*

In my previous career, I edited a memoir by comedian Jen Kirkman called *I Can Barely Take Care of Myself — Tales from A Happy Life Without Kids.* When we were trying to put a title on it, we got a whole lotta feedback from a whole lotta people.

Originally, Jen wanted to call her book *You Will Change Your Mind,* which is the first thing most people say to a woman when she tells them she's "child-free by choice." At this point I don't remember why that was shot down, but I also don't care. I'm stealing it for this chapter title because it applies not *only* to the question of whether to stick a bun in the oven, but to **all kinds of lifestyle choices**

that you might make — and that might make other people uncomfortable enough to lecture you about them.

You know, people like a Dominican tour guide.

# The *elefante* in my uterus

A few months ago my husband and I were with friends,
another married couple, on a tour of Los Haitises National
Park in the Dominican Republic. You get on a boat with a
dozen other tourists and zoom across Samaná Bay, watch
some birds, poke around in a couple of caves, float through
the mangroves, and drink rum. The usual. Our guide,
Rigoberto, was impressively trilingual. He used his English skills to inquire if my girlfriend and I had kids.

"No," my friend replied. "Just cats."

"No," I said, unqualified.

Rigoberto laughed and said to the boat captain in Spanish, *"Hay un problema con sus cosas?"* He was asking if there was
something wrong with our husbands' "stuff" — because of
course that's the only reason two women of fertile age
wouldn't have children waiting back at the dock.

"No," I said, this time in clear Spanish. "*No me gustan los niños.*"

You might think that my responding unambiguously in Rigoberto's native language that I don't like children would have been enough to put the issue to bed, but he *tsk tsked* me (in the universal language) and advised "*Si a tu madre no le gustaban los niños, no estarías aquí.*"

Well, okay, perhaps that's true. If my mother didn't like children I might not be here. And my mother likes children a lot — she not only had two of her own, she taught first and second grade for more than forty years, surrounded by the little fuckers. She always says that if she'd had the financial means she would have had a whole *brood*.

Whereas her mother — my grandmother — did have a brood, but I wouldn't be so sure that was because she liked kids. Maybe she did, but she was also a practicing Catholic married at age twenty in 1946, so you can draw your own conclusions. Either way, by the time she was as old as I am now, my mother's mother had seven children, the oldest fifteen and the youngest two.

And although I can't imagine what it would be like to have even one toddler or one teenager on my watch all day — let alone SEVEN — I know for sure I don't want to try it. I'd rather take my chances with the alligators in the mangroves.

What I didn't bother attempting to explain to Rigoberto was that my mother was the only one of her six siblings to have kids of her own. With a six-year age difference, my brother and I weren't exactly besties, so at family gatherings I socialized among my adult aunts and uncles and spent the occasional holiday or summer weekend with my lone cousin on my father's side. It was totally fine. I never pined for a bigger family or an infant sister to play dress-up on. (I'm afraid I was pretty vocal about not wanting an infant brother, either, once I found out that was what I was getting. Sorry, Tom.)

In any case, I am an almost-forty-year-old woman who has never, ever, not once, wanted to have children. I just don't have the urge to punch that biological clock and my reasons are blissfully uncomplicated, for which I'm grateful. I actually don't think I've ever been so certain of anything *in my entire life*.

So how come lots of people are convinced that I'll change my mind? And what in God's name possesses them to say it to my face?

# How to convert the conventional conversation

It's not as though I haven't taken a number of conventional steps in my life: graduated from high school, went to college, worked a few "career-track" jobs, and got married. The difference between me and a lot of condescending bozos out there is that I don't give a Fig Newton whether anyone else chooses to do it the same, differently, or wearing a gold lamé unitard. You do you.

I also appreciate the freedom to have made — and continue to make — many *unconventional* choices, such as not having children, abandoning my career-track job to move to a third world country, and using Cointreau in my Aperol spritzes instead of a fresh orange slice. Sometimes these choices unnecessarily complicate my life, and sometimes they're a vast improvement over the way anybody else has ever done something.

**What difference does it make to anyone who's not me?**

If a boss doesn't like the way I operate, she can fire me. If a client thinks my unconventional ways aren't for him, he doesn't have to hire me. And anyone else who doesn't like the cut of my jib doesn't have to hang out with me, marry me, or read my books.

However, since you *are* reading my book (Excellent life choices, BTW. Really strong.), it's possible that **"unconventional" describes you, too — or at least some of your thoughts, actions, choices, and sweater vests.**

Or maybe it's a word that Judgy McJudgerson uses to describe you, even if you wouldn't necessarily use it on yourself. Different cow, same block of cheese. Let's slice it up and serve it to him on a decorative platter, shall we?

There are many lifestyle choices that stymie a good chunk of the conventional population. When you declare your intentions toward one of them, you might get some blowback. Such choices include but are not limited to:

**You want to be a sculptor?**
You'll change your mind [as soon as you have another silly whim].

**You want to go vegan?**
You'll change your mind [as soon as you remember that means you can't eat real ice cream].

**You want to be single forever?**

You'll change your mind [as soon as you meet the right guy/girl].

Hey, *I* don't want to sculpt for a living, give up dairy, or have to take out the trash all by myself, but you do you. And I hope you won't take this the wrong way, but **I truly don't care how *you* get from Point A to Point B** — as long as it's not hurting anyone or making a lot of noise when I'm trying to sleep.

Unfortunately, some people just can't take "No I won't" for an answer. Here are some easy ways to shut down the conversation when you have to deal with those people:

| LIFESTYLE CHOICE | RESPONSE TO "YOU'LL CHANGE YOUR MIND" |
| --- | --- |
| Being an artist | "Oh, is that what happened to you, or did you actually *want* to be a tactless busybody when you grew up?" |

| | |
|---|---|
| Celibacy until marriage | "Are you coming on to me?" |
| Not having kids (at 25) | "Right now I'm mostly concerned with keeping the twins perky." |
| Getting a PhD | "Um, that's, 'You'll change your mind, *Doctor.*'" |
| Working for yourself | "I'll be minding my own business and so should you." |
| Not having kids (at 35) | "Nope. Fingers crossed for another thirty years before I pee when I laugh." |
| Going vegetarian/vegan | "Cows don't even get a chance to change *their* minds." |
| Dropping out of school | "Steve Jobs." |

| | |
|---|---|
| Not having kids (over 45) | "Tell it to my ovaries." |
| Marrying young | "Yeah, but the sooner we get hitched, the sooner I can take him for half his assets!" |
| Staying single | "Either way, you're not invited to the wedding." |

Of course, sometimes these Judgy McJudgersons are right. **You could very well change your mind about a previously firmly held belief or decision.** That's usually how divorce works, or how people end up becoming mortgage brokers instead of stand-up comedians. (Though if I may humblebrag here, I got me a mortgage broker who does both.)

But Judgy won't *always* be right, and he certainly shouldn't influence your Major Life Decision-Making with his narrow world view and rude proclamations. A good all-purpose reply is **"Oh dear, it seems I have just changed my mind about having this conversation with you."**

# What if it's not a choice?

Beep, beep! That's my privilege alert going off. (I set it to Hetero, Cis, White Person Tells You What to Do.)*

My extra X chromosome may be my genetic cross to bear, and I may endure discrimination for it (as well as asinine, mildly offensive conversations about my closed-for-business womb), but I have no firsthand knowledge about being gay, lesbian, bisexual, transgender, queer, disabled, African-American, Hispanic, Native American, Muslim, Jewish, or having been born into any other race or ethnicity or creed.

And although NONE OF THOSE THINGS ARE CHOICES, we all know that some assholes think they are, and think you shouldn't be making them. Or that you should be hiding them. Or settling down with a nice girl you met at conversion camp.

Which is to say: I would be remiss in dispensing advice like "You have nothing to lose by being true to

---

* "Cis" is short for "cisgender," a term for people whose gender identity matches the sex they were assigned at birth.

yourself!" or "Just ignore the haters!" if I didn't also **acknowledge the threats to their personal safety when nonhetero, noncis, nonwhite people decide to "do them" on any given day.**

I don't know how that feels, and if it applies to you, I am very sorry you have to deal with this shit. *You Do You* may be a silly self-help book, but I hope it gives you something you're looking for — be it self-acceptance, confidence, solidarity, or a few good laughs.

Whoever you are, I want you to know that I respect your incontrovertible essence, I respect your life choices, and I *won't* try to change your mind about any of them.

Unless they fuck with my sleep, in which case I will cut you.

# You Won't Get Anywhere
# with That Attitude*

*There are plenty of perks
to being a pessimist.*

Among the ways in which we are polar opposites, my husband is relentlessly optimistic, while my glass remains perpetually half empty. This was a source of friction between us for years, until he agreed that letting me work through my daily frustrations with a combination of rage, red wine, and self-pity was better than me wanting to strangle him the next time he told me to look on the bright side. I prefer to stew in a fiery pit of 100-proof feelings rather than douse them with nonalcoholic platitudes. Getting pissed off (and occasionally, as the Brits say, "getting pissed") is how I cope.

Interestingly, my survey revealed that only 37.6 percent of those who took it identify as pessimists. So even adjusting for the fact that I didn't record any important demographic info because I'M NOT A SCIENTIST, MIKE, it would seem that I'm in the minority.

Either way, I think I have something to offer.

**To my fellow Negative Nancys:** Behold! The following section contains cogent arguments to whip out the next time someone says "Why do you always have to be so negative?"

**And to those glass-half-fullers:** You do you (always and forever), but if you're tired of hoping for the best and care to prepare for the worst one of these days, I've got you covered like flood insurance.

# The three little Ps

**Being negative is usually regarded as a bug, not a feature.** It will not surprise you to learn that I couldn't disagree more, and here are three reasons why — all of which start with the letter "P" because I like alliteration, so sue me:

# Productivity

In *Get Your Shit Together,* I debuted my theory "The Power of Negative Thinking"—that is, **how getting mad is great motivation.** Aggravation gets my productivity juices flowing like some kind of magical elixir—it's the Axe Body Spray of "Let's get this over with as soon as humanly fucking possible."

For example, when I allowed myself to acknowledge how unhappy I was in my last job, that helped me get out of it a lot faster than I would have by showing up every day trying to find the bright side of a fluorescent-lit conference room.

A few ways YOU could harness negativity and pessimism to be more productive include:

**Identify the threat:** Assume from the get-go that all people accompanied by small children will have a crisis in the checkout line, and just pick a different register—saving *yourself* a meltdown (and fifteen minutes). Pessimistic? Yes. Practical? You betcha.

**Neutralize the enemy:** Instead of hoping your boyfriend will one day notice the shoe farm he's cultivating by the front door, you could just accept that he won't, harvest a few pairs yourself, and plant them under his pillow. There, now the entryway is clear and you can go back to silently hating other things about Pete.

**Go in guns blazing:** Are your pants too tight? Well, you could sit around waiting for unisex muumuus to become *en vogue* while your waistband chafes at your belly like a lemon zester, or you could get motivated to (a) go on a diet, (b) go to the gym, or (c) buy bigger pants. It's up to you, but I'm not optimistic about the muumuus.

## Planning

Being a pessimist means I always expect the worst to happen, such as during an event or on vacation. That's never going to change (about me), so the least I can do is try to mitigate potential bad outcomes as much as possible, right?

If your glass is running on empty, you know what I'm

talking about. And if you're someone who usually goes with the flow and then gets stuck grinning and bearing it when shit turns sideways, then maybe — just maybe — you might want to give the teeny-tiniest bit of thought to preparing for the worst instead of simply hoping for the best.

Like so:

**Umbrella-ella-ella:** For the life of me I can't understand what would possess a bride — or anyone else, or any party planner in their employ — to count on Mother Nature to smile down on their event. I suppose this might fall under "taking risks," but Lordy, that's a big one (with "bad omen potential" written all over it). No, this pessimist says plan it inside, or at least have a rain plan. Would my wedding have been slightly prettier under wide-open blue sky? Yes, and in fact it did not rain, but that tented courtyard was worth its weight in benzodiazepines.

**A "rain plan" isn't just for rain.** By researching various contingencies, you unfurl a metaphorical umbrella to shield you from all kinds of calamities that might compromise your event or vacation, such as:

| | | |
|---|---|---|
| Parades | → | Devise an alternate route. |
| Major sporting events | → | Reserve hotels wicked far in advance. |
| High winds | → | No hats or tiny dogs allowed. |
| A Royal Wedding | → | Admit defeat; change your date. |
| Locust season | → | Do not go to this place, ever. |

Does it take a little extra energy to run through all the permutations before booking a weekend getaway? Yes, but pessimists understand that an outlay of time and effort on the front end is better than an unexpected scramble on the back end. And any optimist who finds himself trying to sunbathe in Jamaica during hurricane season might soon change his tune from "No worries, mon" to "Why didn't we just *Google* that?"

Hey, if the planned-for bad outcome never comes to pass, then no harm, no foul. At least you controlled the situation as much as you were able so you could enjoy yourself as much as you were able to, too. And your optimistic travel companions can bask in the glow of being right, which is also fun.

**The trick for pessimists is not to spend too much time and energy on — or in my vernacular, "give all your fucks to" — things you *can't* control.** It'll serve you well to research a destination so as not to let your vacation coincide with literally the worst weather that part of the world has to offer — but once you're there, don't get too anxious about the daily forecast. (Obviously you've already researched bad-weather activities, so you have a fallback. Although then again, that's how we ended up at the incomparably boring Heineken factory tour in Amsterdam last summer. A better bad-weather plan would have been "ignore the heavily researched tourist propaganda and drink any other beer at any other bar in the entire city." Oh well, you live, you learn how truly terrible Heineken is.)

## Punctuality

Last but not least (nor late), pessimists are well served when it comes to being on time, whether meeting people or deadlines. Despite having plenty of responsible friends and coworkers, we remain convinced that nobody else will ever show up when they're supposed to, or pull their assigned weight. It's up to us to protect ourselves accordingly, and the first two tips wouldn't hurt optimists, either. (The last one might hit a little too close to home.)

> **The early bird gets out in time for lunch:** Make doctors' appointments for right when the office opens, when they can't already be running late due to flaky clients or overbooking. Why spend any more time than necessary in a dreary, germ-infested waiting room? You're just "waiting" to catch strep.

> **Expect delays:** Any time I have to be somewhere, I just *know* there will be a lane closure, subway malfunction, elevator out of service, or herd of cows in the road, so I give myself an extra ten to twenty minutes to get where I'm going. You'd think this would make me early all the time, twiddling my thumbs until other people saunter in right at the appointed hour. Wrong. I only wind up early about half the time, and the other half, I'm the only one ON time

because nobody else planned ahead for livestock crossings.

[NOTE: Being early does set you up to waste time waiting for other people — but at least you can feel superior *while* waiting. To pass the time, may I suggest a good book about how awesome you are?]

**Time to crack the whip:** My feelings on group projects are well documented in these pages, but if they (the group projects, not the feelings) are unavoidable, getting them done on time is essential to *not prolonging the whole shitshow*. As a pessimist, I know that I have a keen sense of urgency, one that lots of people don't share. I also know that my part will be done early. I will therefore use my extra time to ride YOUR ass to make sure you're finished with the numbers so Gary can plug them into the spreadsheet and then Tina can make the PowerPoint. I will ride Gary's and Tina's asses too, so please don't feel bad. I do me, and you guys get to minimize the time you spend dealing with me. Everybody wins.

# "P" for "Play it close to the vest"

It's all well and good to indulge your pessimistic streak by way of meticulously designed Plans B, C, and D, and even by feeding it the occasional crumb of *I knew this was a bad idea!* But do be careful how often you cry "Anything that can go wrong, will go wrong" — because your loved ones, especially the optimists, are liable to get sick of it.

(Or worse, stop letting you plan the vacations.)

And finally, I suggest not letting your own eminently sensible nature persuade you into getting up in *other people's* business. If they're not worried about shit going wrong and it doesn't affect you, then let 'em make their own decisions and potentially sow their own regrets, meteorologically based or otherwise.

When it comes to letting other people be "wrong" — and per the next chapter — just keep on doing unto them as you would have them do unto you.

# You Will Regret That*

*Says who?*

When I was a college English major we had something called the General Exam, a two-day, eight-hour test you'd take toward the end of your senior year, the scores on which would establish whether you graduated with honors and also what level of honors. Magna, summa, etc. All very important-sounding Latin shit.

Well, you might say I was "generally" aware of the existence of this exam, but not the exact dates on which it would be administered.

By the beginning of my second semester of senior year — January-ish, 2000 — I was in love with a guy I had known for less than six months and I had approximately eleven dollars in my bank account after spending my fall term-time job wages on books, printer cartridges, Au Bon Pain asiago cheese bagels, and an amazing fluorescent red wig that I still own to this day.

I remember my mother coming to visit, and over lunch I told her about my new boyfriend and how I was trying to figure out a way to join him in New Orleans that spring for a music festival, but money was tight, yadda yadda. From her purse, she produced manna from heaven in the form of a belated birthday check from my grandmother.

Handing it to me, she asked if I would be using it to buy a plane ticket.

I couldn't tell if she hoped I'd be able to fulfill my dream of gyrating to Lenny Kravitz and stuffing my face with shrimp po'boys alongside the man I was *sure* I would marry, or if she was testing me to see if I realized that I probably had more pressing expenses. In any case, I answered honestly ("YES!!!") and booked myself a $200 nonrefundable flight to the Big Easy for the first weekend in May.

Sometime in March-ish, my friends started talking about "the Generals"—as though they were actively *preparing* for an upcoming test that had barely registered on my radar in almost four years of school. I really, truly, had not thought about it for a second. I can't explain why or how I missed the memo, but I was shocked—SHOCKED, I tell you—to learn that this exam was due to take place the same weekend I was due to be knee-deep in daiquiris and crawdads. And probably some nookie.

*Well,* I thought, *I can't be in two places at once. And the plane ticket is nonrefundable. And I cannot afford to lose two hundred dollars to this mistake. Also I really want to go to Jazz Fest. Maybe there's a makeup day for the test? Surely other people have conflicts or emergencies that would necessitate some sort of calendrical do-over?*

I poked around on the English department website and didn't find anything that would help me out of my predicament, so I called the person listed as my advisor (to whom I had never before spoken) and explained the situation—that I had foolishly booked air travel before I knew the dates of the exam, I couldn't afford to void the tickets, I really wanted to go on this trip, and could I possibly take the test another time?

In a word: no. (Apparently these dates were made very clear to incoming seniors back in September, and maybe there was some kind of makeup day—my memory is hazy—but either way it was not available to me after I admitted exactly *why* I was going to need that do-over.)

"Okay," I said. "So, um...what happens if I just don't take it?"

"The trip?" said my advisor.

"No, the General Exam. What happens if I just don't take it? Can I still graduate? Can I get honors?"

"Of course you can graduate," she said, at this point sounding a bit peeved. "And yes, with honors from the university if your GPA allows it. But not with honors from the *department*."

She explained that there would be no difference on my diploma either way, but if I wanted to apply to grad school, my score on the General and my standing in the department would matter.

"Oh." (I was not planning to apply to grad school.) "Then I think I just won't take it. There's really no penalty?"

"Not technically, no. But do you really want to prioritize a pleasure trip over this test? I think you're going to regret that."

"Right! Well, thanks for your time. I'll think about it and let you know."

Two months later I was cavorting in New Orleans with my future husband, so I'd say it worked out pretty well, and that I have no regrets.

Except for that last daiquiri. Oof.

# But it feels so right

In "You will change your mind," we talked about what happens when people tell you that you'll never do the thing you say you are GOING to do. Here, we move on to people telling you how you're going to feel AFTER you've done it.

**You want to be a sculptor?**
You'll regret that [when you're dying, penniless and unappreciated].

**You want to go vegan?**
You'll regret that [when people stop inviting you over for dinner].

**You want to be single forever?**

You'll regret that [when you're still swiping left and right at seventy-five].

Both attitudes are condescending, just in different ways. Yay! But the root cause is the same: **You're making choices other people either don't agree with or don't understand** — i.e., what they think of as the WRONG choices, even if said choices are ABSOLUTELY RIGHT for you. Often, this means they're imposing their own *subjective opinions* on you. (See: "You want to be a sculptor?") It's not fun, but you can learn to recognize and work around it, rather than be bullied into **preemptive regret.**

Still, it's important to note the difference between **OBJECTIVELY WRONG, as pertains to morals, ethics, and the law,** and **SUBJECTIVELY WRONG, as a matter of opinion.**

Like, just because I'm all "You do you" doesn't mean I condone being an asshole or a psychopath. (Or a ventriloquist — that shit is freaky.) **If you make the OBJECTIVELY WRONG choice — hurting or exploiting another person,** or breaking the law — you should absolutely be judged for it. In such cases, "wrong" is a fact, not an opinion. So if you're catfishing sad, hairy dudes online or chucking your empty Sprite bottles in the park, cut it out.

(Littering is punishable by both fine and my undying scorn.)

Then there are choices that may not be illegal/immoral, but are still OBJECTIVELY WRONG. Such as making a wrong turn. Not a big deal, but you need to correct it — take three more rights and your next left and you should be fine. If you see your friend about to do something like this, you *should* probably warn them. If you see your enemy about to do it, you may wish to keep mum and enjoy knowing they added an unnecessary forty minutes to their trip. Use your judgment.

SUBJECTIVELY WRONG is more applicable to choices like, say, getting a neck tattoo. When it comes to warning a friend (or foe) against decisions like these, I think we should slow our collective roll. What good is it going to do? Anyone who is seriously contemplating a neck tattoo won't be satisfied until they get one anyway, and if they DO wind up regretting it, they don't need yet another permanent reminder in the form of your "I told you so."

Finally, we have **INNOCENT MISTAKES**, which are a little from column A and a little from column B. Usually the person warning you against making such a choice is injecting their own opinion in the mix (see: neck tattoos), but also has good reason to believe the odds are not in your favor. It's nice of them to warn you, but sometimes you have to take the fall in order to learn the lesson for yourself. I'm reminded of the time I thought it would be easy to slide down the banister at my grandparents' house even though my grampa told me not to and I got stuck on the post at the end of the stairs and my grampa then had to rescue/discipline me.

He was right to have warned me. I was wrong about banisters. And physics.

In short: If someone tells you you're about to do the "wrong" thing and that you "will regret it"—it's useful to think about **whether that's an OBJECTIVE or SUBJECTIVE statement** before you let their judgment stop you from sliding down the banister of life.

Actually I guess that's a bad analogy. How about "before you let them stop you from making your own mistakes and/or living your life any way you damn well please."

**You should try it!**

The opposite of being aggressively warned off something you might like is being aggressively coerced into something you might not. How many times do I have to tell someone I don't eat sushi before they will accept it and allow both of us to move forward with our lives? I KNOW A LOT OF PEOPLE ENJOY SUSHI. I THINK IT SMELLS LIKE THE BOTTOM OF A DOCKWORKER'S SHOE. You can deliver rapturous soliloquies about your favorite things all day long, but if you want to be a good citizen of the world, please stop short of insisting to everyone you meet that they "should" try oysters, neti pots, or anal.

# One wrong doesn't make a regret

For the sake of argument, let's say you did make a wrong decision, in the sense that whatever it was didn't work out the way you'd hoped. That still doesn't mean you'll necessarily regret it. Regret is heavy, man. People write *sonnets* about regret.

Sure, if a former professional boxer currently suffering from concussion-related degenerative brain disease told me I would regret spending fifteen years getting the crap beaten out of me because of what it could do to my health, I would appreciate the heads-up and take it under solid advisement. And then if I did it anyway and eventually found myself suffering from concussion-related degenerative brain disease, I might conclude that I had made the wrong choice, and regret it.

Also the leftover Indian food thing.

But there's a spacious middle ground here — including *Oops, won't do that again* and *Huh, guess that was a bust, oh well, moving on*. Like, I wouldn't say I "regret" putting sauerkraut on my hot dog one time in 2005, but it was definitely the wrong choice for me and now I know better.

---

### This one time, at band camp

As part of my survey, I asked people to share a choice they had made — one which other people had told them they would regret, and which they absolutely did not. The responses ranged from "marrying/not marrying my partner" and "dropping out of school to move abroad" to the more niche "not going to Calgary, Canada, with the marching band after high school graduation." I don't know who you are, you renegade, but since *I* demanded to be released early

---

from my own high school graduation festivities (an all-night bowling/sleepover thing organized by parents to keep their kids from going out and getting drunk), I feel you. All I wanted was to go home and sleep, not get blitzed on Zima, but the chaperones were incredulous and annoyed about it. Still, they let me go. (Have I mentioned that forced interaction with other people is not my thing? And that I'm "difficult?")

## You've got to make your own mistakes, and own the mistakes you make

The other side of the "Accept yourself, then act with confidence" coin is "Act with confidence, then accept the consequences."* In order to feel comfortable making decisions in the first place, you have to feel comfortable getting a few of them wrong. Because you WILL get a few of them wrong. **And when you do, you can't let yourself be permanently sidelined by regret.**

---

* Careful readers will note that this advice harkens back to Helpful Guideline Number Three for Not Being a Psychopath.

More importantly, don't let yourself be paralyzed by *preemptive* regret—foisted upon you by someone who fancies themselves a bit of a soothsayer but in reality, doesn't have an experiential leg to stand on.*

Most of the time, you have to try things for yourself precisely in order to see if they turn out right. If not, you can recalibrate—which we also discussed in the final chapter of Part II, on taking risks. Remember that?

**This book is a veritable Ouroboros of proof that "doing you" is mostly about "just doing it."**

---

* Again, let us revisit the irony of a woman whose book you ostensibly bought for advice, telling you not to take other people's advice. The world works in mysterious ways.

*Is it right or wrong?*

*You won't know unless you have the confidence to take a risk and find out.*

*If you regret your decision, then accept the consequences, swallow the lesson, and start over.*

*With confidence.*

# You Won't Get a Good Job if You Don't Go to College*

*How to succeed at success without really caring what anyone else thinks.

This chapter is for anyone who is, has been, or might someday be tempted to let other people's definition of success determine the course of their life. The title isn't meant to be taken literally (at least not by everyone, or all the time), but it is a useful metaphor for the way society imposes arbitrary judgments on **what constitutes success and how we're meant to achieve it.**

At least *I* think it's a useful metaphor. You can decide for yourself. (That's kind of the point.)

# Success is not one-size-fits-all

Your metaphorical "good job" could be any professional or personal accomplishment. And your metaphorical "college degree" could actually be a literal document that catches the eye of a future employer, or it could be an internship at a theater festival that led you to five Oscar nominations and a net worth of $350 million. Tom Hanks never did graduate from Sacramento State, and he seems to be doing okay.

If you equate success with the accumulation of wealth, you could indeed reach that goal by getting a "good" (aka high-paying) job. You could also do it by saving scrupulously, developing your blackjack skills, making smart investments over time, or marrying rich. (Just sayin'.)

Then again, it may not be wealth alone that represents success in your mind, but what you *do* with it. You could succeed by sending your kids to college or zeroing out your own debt. You could make a down payment on a home, or treat your parents to a fiftieth-anniversary cruise. You might feel the most successful if and when you take all that cash money and give it away to a good cause.

Whatever swabs your deck, sailor!

Or maybe while others prowl the metaphorical high seas for buried treasure, you're on a different voyage entirely — like the person who responded to my survey saying, **"I define success as having flexibility in my life, specifically *because* I don't measure success in terms of climbing a career ladder or making more and more money."**

Lovely. Perhaps you're the same way?

You might be bouncing between credit card bills but feel successful for creating the stable family life you always wanted. Or maybe you've succeeded at a more ephemeral achievement — like summiting a mountain, winning an election, or getting through a five-hour bus ride without peeing your pants. The latter is how I measured the success of every other weekend during my senior year of college.

And if your goal is just to get through the day without crying, it's currently 11:59 p.m., and your eyes are as dry as Norm Macdonald's delivery — then CONGRATU-FUCKINGLATIONS. You have succeeded.

At the end of the day, success is simply the achievement of a goal — any goal — that you set for yourself.

Finding your path to it is not unlike using Google Maps: You type in a destination, it shows you a few different ways to get there, and you pick the one that makes the most sense for you. Less traffic, fewer tolls, scenic route — whatever. You're successful if you get where you intended to go.

| Other things you might succeed at |
|---|
| Being a good listener |
| Having a strong marriage |
| Making people laugh |
| Sobriety |
| Raising good kids |
| Being a community leader |
| Not being a psychopath |
| Leaving the world a cleaner, safer, or merrier place than you found it |
| Staying alive |

But by the same token, you're not "unsuccessful" if you never dialed up a particular destination in the first place, regardless of how popular it may be with others. (I draw your attention once again to the ill-advised Heineken factory tour.)

- If you didn't set the "getting a good job" goal — or if the relative quality of your job is not how you measure success — then I'm guessing you also REALLY enjoy your nights and weekends. Woot!

- If you didn't set the "go to college" goal, you had your reasons, and they won't be costing you an average of $22,693 a year.

- And if you didn't set the "make lots of money" goal, or the "get married" goal, or the "own a home" goal, then *not* doing or *not* having those things doesn't have to cause you stress. Let other people grapple with a complicated tax return, plan a wedding, and gag on monthlies for thirty years. You do you, they do a lot of hyperventilating.

---

**You get a gold star**

Anyone who's read my other books knows I'm big into rewarding myself for good behavior—because if you're always waiting around for other people to pat you on the back, you're likely to wind up standing in the middle of the room for a long time looking like a dumbass. Which is why the price of this book includes ten ways to commemorate and celebrate your own successes (with varying degrees of cost/ effort) when no one else will.

---

You could: Tie one on, dance a jig, upgrade to Extra Space™ Seats, howl at the moon, light up a stogie, binge on *Broad City*, soak those hardworkin' feet, get the extra-large popcorn, pay a visit to Michael Kors, or say "Booyah!" really loudly.

I can personally vouch for nine of these.

# Good hair, don't care

Whenever somebody asked ten-year-old me what I wanted to be when I grew up, my answer was resolute and unwavering: a hairdresser.

My aunt used to take me along to her appointments at a hip salon in my otherwise extremely unhip home state, and I would watch for hours as clients got bleached, colored, frosted, and highlighted; they walked in with shaggy split ends and out with the asymmetrical bobs and pink Mohawks the late eighties were so fond of. It was, I imagined, like hanging out backstage at MTV. One time, my aunt's hairdresser Linda — who was at that point the coolest chick I'd ever met and still ranks in the top ten — ran a combful of semipermanent purple dye over my brown hair. You could hardly see it, but I felt like Cyndi **fucking** Lauper when I walked into school that week.

I'd caught the bug, and it stayed with me for life. Since then I've been black-, burgundy-, and red-haired, peroxide blond, Mrs. Mia Wallace from *Pulp Fiction* and Mia Farrow in *Rosemary's Baby*. Many hairstylists in New England, New York, and the Dominican Republic have had their way with my Visa card.

But one day when I was probably twelve or thirteen, a friend of my parents asked me that innocent question about my career plans, and she definitely didn't like the answer. It was as though I'd told her I intended to grow up to be a cardsharp or a foot fetishist. She urged me to consider how much "more" I could do with my life than frost tips and get high on perm fumes.

"Don't you want to go to college?" she asked.

At the time I'm not sure I even knew whether you needed to go to college to become a hairdresser. I hadn't given it much thought. I wouldn't have been *opposed* to the idea, since "college" was also where, I'd been reliably informed, you could stay up as late as you wanted and eat dinner out of vending machines. But the reason I hadn't given it much thought was because **"what I want to be when I grow up" wasn't dependent on "how I would get there."**

I just wanted to do hair.

It's not that I don't understand where this woman was coming from. But her knee-jerk disapproval of a future that I'd been happily imagining for myself was like a nick to the earlobes with the business end of the shears. It stung, and the feeling stayed with me. I started to think it wouldn't be "okay" if I became a hairdresser like Linda. That people would be disappointed in me for choosing the kooky, fun camaraderie of a hair salon over, say, the solitary intellectual rigor of higher education.

Gradually the idea of being a hairdresser faded away like a perfect ombré, and I pointed myself toward academia — thinking I'd get a master's and a PhD and become a professor. Think again! (As you know, by the time I encountered the General Exam, I'd already revised that plan.) A few false starts — an internet boom gig that went bust, six months making minimum wage at a bookstore, a stint as a VIP greeter on Broadway\*—and I found my groove as a book editor. Fifteen years later, I threw it all away to make some radical changes and work for myself, and most recently, became a writer whose calling card is "words that can't be printed in the *New York Times*."

My point is, in 1991, none of us had any idea what I would "grow up" to be, so why did it matter so much to my parents' friend that she would try to dissuade me from a path I was, at the time, really excited about?

Clearly she thought she was helping—the same way everyone who tells me I'll regret not having children thinks they're doing me a favor, saving me from myself.

But most of us don't need saving.

**We just need permission to be ourselves, make our own decisions and mistakes, and revel in our own success, whatever that means to us.**

It's time to grant that permission to your own damn self. Because living your life according to other people's definitions of success is the same as living your life according

---

\* There are some things you cannot un-see, and Liza Minnelli's camel toe is one of them.

to other people's dreams, other people's fears, and other people's notions of risk and regret. That's not helping anybody.

And in the end, the only person it *hurts* when you shape your life according to other people's standards?

# YOU.

Carry on.

# You Will Never
# Live that Down*

*Yes you will. Go ahead and let
your freak flag fly.*

You might say I have a thing for traffic cones.

I am in possession of more than one photo of myself wearing a traffic cone as a hat. One of them is from New Year's Eve 2012. I was walking home with friends from a party in Brooklyn and fell behind because I was focused on appropriating a cone and getting it onto my head before shouting for someone to turn around and take a picture. It fell completely down over my face and when he took in the scene, my husband said, "You know dogs have peed against that, right?"

What can I say? I'm committed to my art.

I'm also really into something I call "frolicking." Every once in a while I get the urge to go skipping along — on the pavement, down the beach, in someone else's yard (other people might call this "trespassing")—and have my own private dance party. A good frolic gets the sad out of you, as Marlo Thomas might say, and it's also a nice, low-impact workout.*

I have "borrowed" an inflatable dolphin from a hotel gift shop and "danced" with it to Calvin Harris's "Feel So Close" in front of the crowd at an expensive fund-raiser. I have attempted (and failed) to shinny up a palm tree to impress a three-year-old girl. I once played Lust in my friends' Seven Deadly Sins Halloween pageant and ate grapes off the bosoms of the girl who played Gluttony. I've got photo- or videographic proof of all these activities, and there's a lot more where those came from.

These are all things I chose to do, knowing how weird they might look or how much evidence might one

---

* To date, my husband has prevented me from frolicking on the set of *Survivor: Turkey*, which films in our town in the Dominican Republic. Someday I will sweet-talk both him *and* the armed guard who patrols the grounds into letting me at least photo bomb an immunity idol.

day be used against me in the court of YouTube. Sometimes it's because I'm tipsy. Okay, a lot of the time. But I'm also not shy about being weird, because it's fun, it's funny, and it's who I am — the Janus face of my type A, recovering-perfectionist, takes-most-shit-too-seriously personality. Plus, as you've probably inferred from earlier stories about my semirepressed adolescence of people-pleasing and conformity — I've got a lot of lost time to make up for.

Maybe you do too?

## Wacky with a chance of goofballs

At this point in our narrative, we've discussed unconventional life choices, risk, fear, and regret; and in Part IV, we'll hack into the thorny underbrush of family relations, physical appearance, and mental health. So I'm thinking now's a good time to enjoy a mental palate cleanser, and spend the final chapter of Part III **getting comfortable with getting weird**.

Strange. Quirky. Eccentric. The whole shebang. Letting that tiger out of the cage and getting those freak flags rippling on the breeze.

WHO'S WITH ME?!?

(Extra points if you just said "I am!" out loud in a crowded waiting room or on public transportation.)

Excellent. First, some parameters:

- Plain old day-to-day weirdness is different from "making unconventional life choices." The former is about discrete acts of nonconformity and odd-ball lunacy, whereas the latter encompasses entire unusual or unpopular paradigms for living — whether vis-à-vis a career path, family planning, extreme fitness, tiny house, etc.

- Both, however, are *choices*. When I say someone is "being weird," I mean they are making an active, conscious choice to be, do, and/or say peculiar things that fall outside society's established norms. I'm not saying those norms are always rational or justified, just that we all know they exist. Such norms include not talking about yourself in the third person, not showing up in costume to a non-costume party, and not wearing pilfered construction equipment on your head.

- Finally, I think of "being weird" as behavior that isn't hurting anybody else. Like that guy on the subway platform dancing a tango with a life-sized doll Velcroed to his wrists and ankles. Who's he hurting? No one. You do you, guy dancing a tango with a life-sized doll Velcroed to your wrists and ankles. Weirdness is different from the nonnegotiable clauses in the social contract that I mentioned in Part I, such as bestowing the gift of your junk on a band of unsuspecting carolers. There is no moral, ethical, or legal reason *not* to be weird. There is only Judgy McJudgerson, waiting in the wings to smirk at you. (Frankly, I wouldn't be surprised if Judgy talks about Judgy in the third person.)

**With those ground rules established, I do declare that we, as a society, should celebrate weirdness in all its forms — and that the right to be weird should be**

**inalienable** — just like the right to life, liberty, and the pursuit of happiness.*

This is what the phrase "You do you" was meant for!

If everyone on earth responded to acts of well-intentioned weirdness with acceptance and encouragement, we'd all be having a lot more fun, with a generous dollop of self-confidence. (And you don't have to be weird yourself if you don't want to, but you can be tolerant of others and get some free entertainment out of the deal. What do you have against whimsy?)

I myself am blessed by the friendship of a bunch of weird weirdos who accepted me into their lives and nurtured my frolicking streak over time. If you are one of us, I want you to know in no uncertain terms:

**You are awesome and there is nothing wrong with you.**

If you are not one of us, know this:

**You could be.**

---

* Or for any Canadians who might be reading: The right to feel superior to Americans with regard to your nationalized health care system and the boyish good looks of your fearless leader.

# Making it weird

The rest of this chapter is split into three parts.

The first is for people who already self-identify as weird and came here looking for validation and spiritual high fives;

The second is for people whose freak flag flies at half-mast — they have a propensity for weird but need help standing strong in the face of pressure to reel it in;

And the third is for those who are what I like to call "weird-curious"...and who might be wondering how they can join the party.

## Freak flag: flying high

Some folks are totally comfortable in their weirdness. My friend Bryan, for example, wears a terry-cloth headband at all times and often speaks in Zen koans. My buddy Steve has a brown belt in scatological humor. And one of my college professors used to introduce herself to people and then act out their zodiac signs via interpretive dance.

If you're weird and you know it — and you're out there doing you on a daily basis — there must be some reason you haven't backed down or buttoned up in the face of societal pressure to do so. It's possible that you live in an unusually accepting environment, perhaps among carnies or nursery school teachers. It's possible that you read my first book and no longer give a fuck about what anybody else thinks. Or perhaps, in addition to being weird, you're already exceptionally confident in your weirdness. Regardless, you don't need my validation.

### 5 signs you might already be weird

You consider every Wednesday an opportunity to wear white tie and tails.

You talk to animals and also talk back *as* the animals in funny voices.

You never met a Juggalo you didn't like.

You have ninety-nine problems, but imperfectly enunciated Klingon ain't one.

You prefer Cool Ranch Doritos to Nacho Cheese. (In this case, you are not only weird, you're also a communist.)

Instead, please accept this drawing of a traffic cone wearing a traffic cone on its head, a gift from me to you:

## Freak flag: half-mast

Then there are folks who know they're weird and some-times flaunt it, but afterward they feel judged and criti-cized. If this is you, **you're living in the purgatory of being yourself without feeling *good* about being your-self.** In my humble opinion, that cycle of embarrassment-shame-repression is a lot worse than the occasional unwelcome snicker or dirty look from a stranger.

How about a little **mental redecorating** to help you break that cycle?

Step 1: Identify your "flaws."

Step 2: Refresh the way you look at and/or deal with them.

If your "flaw" is a penchant for outlandish outfits or elaborate maquillage, well, that didn't stop Gene Simmons! Instead of treating your favorite wardrobe items or cosmetics like the incense you only light when you're feeling frisky, you could start burning that stick of Exotic Sandalwood all day every day. Eventually, people will get used to it. (They might even secretly wish they smelled like you.)

Or perhaps your sense of humor, like a scary clown painting in the powder room, can be unsettling to unsuspecting guests. You don't have to replace it with a Norman Rockwell print, but you could relocate your schtick to the basement game room where your most fun friends are likely to encounter it in a relaxed, receptive mood. Let's just say I've been on the delivering end of a few volleys that didn't land, and now I only make merkin jokes in front of people with a background in fifteenth-century prostitution and/or pubic lice. Gets 'em every time.

**By rearranging your mental décor, you make it easier and more pleasant to get through your own life — and for the people *in* your life to do so too.**


## Freak flag: low and tight

Finally, let's say you don't yet self-describe as weird, but more "weird-curious." I would love to be of assistance on your journey of self-discovery. For starters, here are three easy ways to let loose and channel your inner weirdo.

### Pretend you're a toddler

The last time you didn't care about what other people thought of you was probably when you were still in diapers, right? Little kids are blissfully unaware of society's capacity for judgment — they make up songs, wear pipe cleaners as jewelry, and talk to inanimate objects (not to mention, frolic to their hearts' content).

**EXERCISE:** Take a crash course in weird by following a two-year-old around for a few hours and doing whatever he does. Point at birds while making pig noises; wear a bucket on your head while using a plastic rake as a scepter; laugh maniacally at your own flatulence. Literal baby steps.

### Pretend you're a celebrity

Another [relatively] consequence-free subset of the weirdo population: your favorite pop stars, actors, fashion designers, YouTubers, and athletes. Name one reason why Lady Gaga can wear a gown made of raw beef and you can't. Or why Chad Johnson can legally change his last name to "Ocho Cinco" and you can't. (Hint: the reason is "confidence.") People either already admire celebrities and therefore accept their eccentricities, or those eccentricities form the basis for the admiration in the first place. So you're not a celebrity — so what? That doesn't mean you can't indulge in a little freedom of expression.

**EXERCISE:** The next time you go out to dinner, offer to take selfies with fellow patrons as though you *are* famous. That's superweird, yet if you do it with confidence, people won't even realize it. They will literally be begging you for more.

## Pretend you're alone

If you're looking for a loophole in the social contract, being by yourself is it. There's nobody to please, bow down, or cater to. Nobody to see you shake a tail feather, hear you harmonize, or critique your Hammer Dance. But if you love to boogie down and sing along, who says you have to limit those feel-good vibes to "when other people aren't watching?"

> **EXERCISE:** Start slow, by pretending you're alone even when you aren't. For example: alone in your car, but pulled up to a stoplight at a busy intersection with the windows down; alone on a balcony or rooftop, but with other people milling below; or alone in a bathroom stall at a busy bar or restaurant. (Once when I was putting on lipstick, I heard a woman pee while belting out "R-e-s-p-e-c-t." If that isn't a self-fulfilling prophecy, I don't know what is.) Eventually, you'll

get the hang of being weird in public. It's all about granting your inner monologue its outside voice, regardless of who's there to listen.

Finally, one last piece of unconventional wisdom from the woman who recently copped, in print, to putting traffic cones on her head and enjoying semiregular frolicking sessions:

**Acknowledging and acting on your own weirdness gives you power.**

How? Because not only does acceptance breed confidence, confidence *itself* is disarming.

Why? Because people are easily manipulated.

(What? It's true.)

And doing anything on purpose, with purpose, is the best way to hide in plain sight.

# IV

## SHOULDS &
## SHOULDN'TS:
Much too much obliged

Welcome to the fourth and final part of *You Do You*. After this, it's just a zippy epilogue that will neatly sum up the ideas of the book and then drop a philosophical bombshell to inform your future doing-you practices well after the last page is turned.

But no peeking. We still have five more amendments to go — ones which modify the especially soul-crushing clauses born of **obligation.**

This is my JAM, guys.

I began publicly expressing my disdain for obligation in *The Life-Changing Magic of Not Giving a Fuck,* in which I said that feeling obligated to do (or not do) something was the worst possible reason to do (or not do) something. I stand by that assessment. In that book, I argued that the best way to balance your Fuck Budget and avoid Fuck Overload™ is to **allocate your time, energy, and money to what you *want* to do rather than what you feel *obligated* to do.**

As for the nonnegotiable fucks that you have to give whether you like it or not?

I dealt with those in *Get Your Shit Together,* where I explained how to knock out that "must do" stuff so you can — once again, with feeling — focus on doing what you really want, instead of only what you feel *obligated* to do on any given day.

The first two entries in the no-fucks-given guide canon stress the importance of "joy over annoy" and "choice over obligation." By now, I'm sure you realize *You Do You* is a peacock of identical plumage. (That's no accident — everybody loves a three-peat.)

In this book, I'm going to **concentrate on five *specific* cultural obligations that are condescending, unnecessarily limiting, and/or profoundly stupid.** These clauses of the social contract deal in the imperative, a tense that makes me very tense.

Part IV opens with the chapter **"You should always put family first,"** a nod to all the black sheep grazing calmly at the fringes of the yard while their fuzzy white brethren point hooves and *baa, baa* behind their backs. I'll also talk about **chosen family**, and the benefits of sloughing off your kin to seek out your own kind — forming bonds that inspire you to drop everything for someone you love who doesn't even share your genetic profile. Imagine that!

Next, in **"You shouldn't act so crazy,"** we'll don our

aptly named pants to address the stigma surrounding anxiety and other forms of mental illness. I speak from experience when I say that availing yourself of proud, public self-care is a million times healthier than enduring a private mental breakdown. Probably a billion, but I was an English major, I don't count that high.

In **"You should smile more,"** I'll examine the fetishization of niceness with regard to *looking, acting,* and *the saying of things.* I don't support mouthing off, making enemies, and being mean for no good reason. But nor should you feel compelled to present a veneer of beatific calm to the world when inside, you're minorly irritated or majorly pissed off.

(Unless you are Catherine, Duchess of Cambridge. You made your bed, girl, but thanks for reading!)

Afterward, we'll snuggle up to body image issues in **"You shouldn't eat that,"** and I'll explain why they're the same as every other issue you're having. And finally, in **"You should check your ego at the door,"** I'll argue that [unless you are the blustering, incompetent commander-in-chief of the world's most fearsome army, dangling your diminutive trigger finger over the nuclear codes] a big ego is no liability; it's actually your biggest asset.

We'll wrap up *You Do You* with a thorough stroking of the asset in question (which will have already swollen in size like the Grinch's heart as you've absorbed the last couple hundred pages of positive reinforcement).

Remember, guys: THERE IS NOTHING WRONG WITH YOU.

I hate to be pushy, but you should listen to me on this.

# You Should Always Put Family First *

*First runner-up is okay too.*

The sentiment *Family comes first* — and its implied addendum, *no matter what* — is an aspect of the social contract at which I've always taken umbrage. That's not because I don't love my family. I do, and I think most of them are pretty fond of me, too. But I believe that **love and respect should be consistently earned** — not granted in perpetuity on the basis of having passed a single DNA test.

Sure, biologically speaking it makes sense for families to "stick together through thick and thin" so that their line is more likely to survive and thrive. That's Evolution 101, and also the plot of all the *Godfather* movies. And yeah, I see why parents who showed unconditional love and loyalty to their helpless child while raising him up into the world might expect similar unconditional love and loyalty when they need taking care of *by* said child later in life.*

Look, I may be an antisocial anti-guru, but I'm not an asshole. **If your family loves you and treats you with respect, love and treat them with respect right back.** That makes total sense! I just happen to think the same should go for anyone you love and respect, not just the ones who populate your Ancestry.com account — and consequently, that **family doesn't *always* deserve *automatic* top billing**.

The first section of this chapter is an **ode to black sheep** — those of us who are less a chip off the old block and more a large chunk, excised, rotated, and then reaffixed at an odd angle. If this doesn't apply to you, or if you're one of those sheeple but you and your family have achieved barnyard détente, that's terrific. Next time I need guest gurus on the book tour, I'll give you a ring.

The second is about **making and executing tough choices when it comes to spending time with nonfamily**

---

* I would point out that this child didn't ask to be born in the first place, but that's exactly the kind of specious argument Amelia from Amazon.com would have a field day with, and I don't need to give her any live ammo. (You'll meet Amelia in a couple of chapters.)

**over family, and then not feeling bad about it.** "No" is an acceptable answer, even on the RSVP card to your cousin Jennifer's wedding.

The third section is **an antidote to all my anti-guruing.** I know you might be reading this book because I have the temerity to say what you've been thinking—but have thus far been unable or afraid to express—about the many ways in which other people drive you up the goddamn wall. I'm happy to provide this service. But occasionally, I also like to remind my readers that there's a lot to love about their lives, such as their wonderful friends—aka their chosen family. At the end of this chapter, we'll celebrate them!

# Bye, bye, black sheep

As you may know, the term "black sheep" originally referenced someone who had brought disgrace or disrepute upon their family. A troublemaker and/or an embarrassment— perhaps getting pregnant out of wedlock or getting caught becoming a little too familiar with an actual sheep on the neighbor's property.

You do ewe, so to speak.*

The phrase has evolved to mean not fitting in with (and perhaps being shunned by) the rest of one's family for any reason, not necessarily having gone so far as to bring disgrace or disrepute. If you're considered by yourself or others to be the "black sheep," it may simply be that you don't like the same things your siblings like or value the same things your parents value, or that your freak flag flies a little (or a lot) higher than theirs.

> *Why doesn't Steffie want to practice the religion the rest of us submitted blindly to from birth?*

> *Why doesn't Charles own a decent tie?*

> *We just don't understand how Miriam gets through the day with all those opinions about reproductive rights!*

Maybe, alone among your cousins, you reject the view that infants should be invited to weddings. Maybe you opted out of the last three family reunions because fruit punch and passive-aggression aren't your thing. (Definitely your aunt Kathy's thing, but not yours. She's almost

---

* This is why they pay me the big bucks, people.

as into Lowest Common Denominator Living as she is into proselytizing for her Baptist Book Club.)

Personally, I'm lucky to have an accepting clan. (Either that, or 90 percent accepting and 10 percent can't be bothered to give a fuck about what I'm up to, which is also fine.) In that sense, this is probably the least personal section of *You Do You,* but it's by no means the least relevant to many readers — especially the 40 percent of respondents who identified as black sheep in my survey.

If you're feeling down-and-outcast by your family's judgment, I have good news: There's no need to dye your metaphorical wool to fit in with the flock, or even to butt horns about it.*

Instead, I recommend just...*agreeing* with them.

Counterintuitive, I know, but hear me out. (**Remember: Mental redecorating doesn't change *who you are,* only *how you cope.*)**

Technically, what they're saying is true, right? Your mental wall of framed progressive protest posters *wouldn't* belong in the staunchly conservative mental house you grew up in. Your mental foyer, empty of belief in a higher

---

* Yes, I am bleating this metaphor to death.

power, *doesn't* mimic your aunt Kathy's mental shrine to her Lord and Savior. And your mental duvet cover sees quite a bit more action than your sister Lucy's ever has.

So what. It's your house.

**The sooner you accept that, stop feeling bad about it, and start feeling confident in your own little branch of the family tree — the sooner you will truly be singular among your relatives.**

You'll be the unique, atypical, exceptional "black sheep" of the damn family precisely BECAUSE you're the only one well adjusted enough to know that there is nothing wrong with you.

See what I did there?

And if you're looking to spruce up the foyer, did you know that dart boards can be custom-made using family photos? Such as, I don't know, one of Aunt Kathy's smug face? Just an idea.

# Reclaiming your time

In my survey, I asked "How much time do you spend with your family that you wish you didn't?" Only a third of responders said "None, I always love being with them." The other 66 percent confessed to feeling in some way overburdened by togetherness, and nearly 10 percent clicked "A LOT."

Well, far be it from me to deprive you and your families of the joy of or barely disguised tolerance for your presence, but I think I can be of assistance in bringing these numbers to a slightly more equitable level.

As I said, in *You Do You* we're not talking total elimination. (I have a different book for that.) Here, we're going to assume that 66 percent of you are more than happy to spend some fuck bucks on your family—just not quite so *many*, or quite so *often*.

You genuinely want to make lunch plans and go to their parties and visit them in prison, but you don't enjoy **feeling *obligated* to kick them to the top of a crowded list of want-to-do stuff** just because society (or Grandma) tells you that family should always come first.

Well, in my opinion, sharing a last name or a gene pool is right up there with "I saw it on *Tosh.0*" as a good reason to do something. But I get it: **Letting arbitrary**

**factors decide for you is easier than making tough choices on your own.** (And I don't mean "Your mother and your friend Mandy are drowning and you can only save one of them. Who do you choose?" Sadistic hypotheticals are the purview of psychopaths and philosophy majors, neither of whom has anything to brag about in the way of good decision-making.)

I'm talking about choices like going to a nonfamily event over a family one — I just don't think they actually *need* to be so tough. For the sake of argument, and to make sure everyone's blood is set to boil, let's call them both weddings.

## There can be only one. (It doesn't have to be your cousin Jennifer.)

Let's say that hypothetically, your cousin Jen's ceremony in Boston is being held opposite your friend Tito's blowout in Austin.

You love them both, you'd love to attend both, and both are theoretically once-in-a-lifetime events (although, knowing Tito…). But you can't be in two places at once, even just once in your lifetime.

And I know you. Not all shindigs are created equal, and no matter how much you love your family and friends, you *do* have a front-runner. Just like your mom has a favorite kid.

So if you're really close to Cousin Jen and psyched about the all-you-can-eat raw bar Uncle Joe is shelling out for at Legal Sea Foods, AND that's the party you'd truly rather attend, the decision is easy. You can let Tito down gently with a "Hey, man, I really wish I could be there but, you know — *family.*" He'll never know the difference.

But what if you'd rather spend your weekend guzzling IPAs and BBQ on Tito's behalf in Austin? In that case, my guess is you're going to feel much more conflicted about choosing Tito's party over Jen's because, you know — *family.* And, just another wild guess here: **You're likely to go with your second choice and forever hold your peace.**

Poor Tito.

And poor you.

(More brisket for everyone else, though.)

Well, I say SPEAK NOW, COWBOY. Deliver a perfectly reasonable no to Jenny, yes to Tito, and shine up your spurs, because you're going to Texas!

---

### Altar-nate plans

By the way, marriage—or any romantic partnership—is Exhibit A for the benefits of going outside the bloodline. The person who pledged to be by your side for better or worse might be your escape from an untenable family situation, or at least provide you shelter from the occasional Christmas-morning storm. Not only do you get to spend your days and nights with someone you actively chose (and who actively chose you)—you also, should you wish, have the opportunity to raise new people together with your actively chosen values. And then those people will have the chance to do the same one day, which is pretty cool. There's a reason incest died a slow, genetically compromised death in the modern world.

---

If I may beat this lesson into the ground like a rusty croquet wicket: **It's okay to prioritize choice over a sense of obligation.** Probably more than a few people (<waves to Amelia from Amazon>) will read that last sentence and either sympathize with my parents or wonder what's wrong with them that they produced such a selfish, heartless bitch of a daughter.

*Perhaps she was raised among feral cats? They're pretty stand-offish. It's plausible.*

As it happens, my mother and father are both quite family-oriented (and neither is a feral cat). They're close to their parents and siblings; they've willingly submitted to a fair amount of drama and trauma on behalf of both; and they clearly love having their own kids around even if their eldest is a potty-mouthed harpy. But the thing is — AND TO THEIR CREDIT — my parents have never made me feel obligated to do anything in the name of family. They know who I am: someone who does what she wants, when and why she wants, while being totally upfront about it.

They accept me. Or maybe they're afraid of me. All I know is, we get along a lot better than other families I know who are up each other's butts about putting each other first — and therefore our quality time together is actual quality, not a hostage situation.

Again, I count myself lucky on this score. But if you have family members who feel entitled to your time and who can't understand why you would *ever* put anyone else first, I think I can help. As I've said, "No" is an acceptable answer (and a complete sentence), but if that doesn't work, there are other ways to get your point across.

### 5 ways to talk to your family about choosing other people over them

1. Tell Grandma you love her and hope her parakeet Mabel has a great birthday party, but you love the idea of swinging with your friends Kevin and Jill at their anniversary bash at Sandals more. None of you will speak of this again.
2. Explain your totally valid excuse for skipping your sister's church picnic. Via FaceTime, from the toilet. Now she'll be the one making totally valid excuses to get off the call.
3. Say you were excited to join your parents at their Qigong retreat over the holiday weekend, but your boyfriend got tickets to Beyoncé AND you think he might be proposing. They will be mollified by the idea of adding a son-in-law they can guilt into future Qigong retreats but feel awkward about saying anything if he *doesn't* put a ring on it.
4. Reassure your uncle Bert that his annual backyard Sausage Fest was just barely edged out by the chance to go in on a beach house share with a group of people you barely know who can procure *amazing* weed.
5. Relay your decision in spoken word poetry. Everyone will promptly uninvite you from everything.

You love these people. You respect them. But you also have a life outside the family unit and that's okay — your parents, grandparents, siblings, aunts, uncles, and cousins can stand to come in second sometimes.

Except if you need an organ replacement, in which case they should always be your first call.

# I choo-choo-choose you

But hey, I'm not just here to gripe and grumble and dash off uncomfortably accurate hypotheticals about your relationship with your cousin Jennifer! I'm also into rewarding people who appreciate you for you — so let's end this chapter on a high note and give friends like Tito their time in the sun.

Tito is someone you met once and chose to keep hanging out with of your own volition, under zero obligation. Maybe he was your next-door neighbor growing up and you bonded early. Maybe you met him at summer camp, or in college. Maybe he answered your Craigslist ad for a roommate and he didn't drug and assault you, so you were like *Awesome, I could totally be friends with this guy!*

In any case, Tito really gets you.

He knows you become inordinately excited about new *Sharknado* movies and you don't give a fuck about craft beer. He shares your sense of humor, which is a rare quality in people who are not long-haul truckers. He doesn't always text back right away, but you know he's there for you. Lately he may be a little hurt that you're not coming to his wedding, given that you're best friends and he's never even heard you mention your cousin Jennifer, but he'll come around, **because friends don't guilt friends into doing shit they can't or don't want to do.**

And you really get Tito.

You know that once he starts talking about sabermetrics, there's no stopping him. You put up with it because you like geeking out about stuff too, and that's part of what makes you compatible. (You might be a little more devoted to your collection of vintage belt buckles than is strictly healthy.) It's easy to be around Tito. You don't have to pretend you're interested in the minutiae of his life, because you genuinely are.

The fact is, you chose Tito and Tito chose you. **It's a privilege to have friends like these — they don't get automatically handed out at birth.** Appreciate them. Support them. Go ahead and put them first.

The friends who don't judge you for choosing what's best for you are the ones you'll want to keep closer than anyone. And honestly? Tito's idea of what's best for you is probably more in line with your own than, say, that of someone you would never befriend in a million years but will wind up sharing space in a mausoleum with someday because, you know — *family*.

# You Shouldn't Act So Crazy*

*I kept a litter box under my
desk for a year and I turned out okay.*

When I was cleaning out our Brooklyn apartment in preparation for the big tropical move, I uncovered a number of items that I'd forgotten we owned. Among them: the plush vulva puppet gifted to me by a former author, tucked away in a hatbox; the "scorpion bowl"—a glass pipe shaped like its arachnoid namesake that we'd acquired on a family vacation to Mexico; and one wok, never used.

Under the bed, I found a cardboard box containing a small painting of an ocean view, framed in white like the window of someone's beach house, and a piece of pock-marked driftwood.

You might be wondering why I, a person who considers decluttering to be foreplay and who foregoes sentimentality related to objects that have outlived their usefulness, would have held on to this box? Why indeed. It was a bona fide reliquary, wrapped in packing tape and stuffed with vivid memories of the worst time in my life and one of the nicest things anyone has ever done for me.

# Leave your biofeedback at the tone

After several years of undiagnosed symptoms — including blinding headaches, stomach cramps, shortness of breath, and hives (*Look! They're spreading all over her body like the mounds of some exotic miniature skin gopher!*) — when I was thirty-one, I finally had my first full-blown panic attack. Or at least I had a panic attack that was so bad it was impossible to ignore; I think there were probably a couple of mini ones in my past, like the tremors that presage a major earthquake.

That terrible, horrible, no-good, very bad day resulted in me finally going to a doctor. And eventually finally listening to that doctor when she said I should try biofeedback as a treatment for the root cause(s) of my anxiety, rather than taking fistfuls of pain, nausea, and antihistamine meds to treat the symptoms.

I was skeptical. *Biofeedback? What the fuck is that? Sounds like a fancy word for "YOU CRAZY, WOMAN."*

And once I found out what biofeedback was — having electrodes taped to my arm while the doctor asked me questions about my feelings and tracked my stress response on a monitor — I was even more wary. Painkillers and Zantac I understood. Those were treating my physical ailments. This course of action sounded a lot more like "mental help," and boy oh boy I did not want to think I needed that.

Well, it is a VERY GOOD THING that I got over myself and gave it a shot. (Several contiguous months of pain and suffering will do that to a girl.)

The first session was eye-opening. My doctor patiently explained what the panic response is, how thoughts and perceived threats can manifest as physical reactions, and that there was nothing "crazy" about the way I'd been feeling.

Still, I was loathe to accept that any part of my brain — my big, beautiful, formerly dependable brain — could betray me, and it took a few visits to accept and process what she was saying. If you or anyone you know is going through similar mental gymnastics accompanied by physical suffering, I hope my talking about it openly will help you reach that conclusion faster than I did.

Eventually, she taught me how to "down-regulate" with breathing and other exercises. And she taught me that there was no more reason for me to feel like a failure because I couldn't control my fight-or-flight response than for RuPaul to feel bad about being so naturally goddamn fierce.

---

### I'm not a doctor, I don't even play one on TV, please don't sue me.

Now seems like a good time to state unequivocally that the advice in this chapter is based on my personal struggles with generalized anxiety and panic disorder, and that while I've known many people with these and other diagnoses of mental illness, both milder and more severe, I don't pretend to be able to speak for them or for you. There are many fantastic books that address mental health and wellness in both a more expansive and a more medically sound way than this one. All I can do is tell you what I've experienced and what I've learned, and maybe if you apply some of that to your life, things will improve.

As an old boss of mine used to say, "Hey, it's better than a kick in the teeth."

---

**I had been wrong to think that a mental health problem was any different from a physical problem that I would have gladly, unashamedly sought treatment for.**

So what does all of this have to do with that driftwood under my bed? Patience, my pretties.

# Life's a beach*

So, among the assignments my [actual, accredited] doctor handed out was to list a few things that made me feel happy and calm and then incorporate those things into my life as much as possible. It might sound silly (especially when I tell you what my things were), but

a) it really worked

b) the whole point of this chapter is to NOT deprive yourself of help, health, and happiness just because it might seem "silly" — to yourself or anyone else.

---

* (and then everybody dies)

We can't let stigma win. It's *such* an insufferable prick.

One item on my list was "trashy magazines." For someone who spent her professional life reading and thinking critically every day, zoning out to *Us Weekly* was a balm for my overtaxed frontal lobe. My husband promptly bought me a subscription. (His application for sainthood is still processing, though I signed off on it years ago.)

Also ranking high: bubble baths. The fact that we had a tub in our Brooklyn apartment for five years and I didn't start using it until it was *prescribed* to me, well, I count that as a gross personal failure.

But the big one — the thing I love to do most in the world and that decreases my stress level like a pitcher of margaritas decreases my ability to keep my shirt on — is to sit in the sun, looking at the ocean, with my feet in the sand. I've since made this a permanent condition, but at the time I didn't have a lot of opportunities to beach it up. Certainly not during the workday, the very hours that were constantly sabotaging my nervous system.

So, I went out and bought myself a litter box.

Yes — I, a human woman, purchased a cat toilet for personal use. Desperate times call for desperate measures, guys and gals. I smuggled it into my office along with ten containers of "craft sand" from an art supply store in Midtown Manhattan, set it up under my desk, and periodically (and surreptitiously) slipped off my heels to smother my feet in a simulated beach.

And it worked! But it didn't stay surreptitious for long.

I don't know how I thought nobody would notice A FUCKING LITTER BOX in my office, but **stigma is a powerful catalyst for denial.** Eventually my assistant asked me about it. She'd been out the day of my panic attack, so I told her the whole story and all about my list of silly, calming things.

The next day, I came in to work to find a surprise tableau on the shelf above my computer monitor: a framed painting of a beach scene and, to the right, a piece of bleached driftwood and a kit of "air plants" meant to be stuffed into the wood's natural holes, little sprigs designed to survive under even the harshest of circumstances.

My assistant looked at me brightly. "Now you have a beach to look at when you put your feet in the sand," she said.

Tears of gratitude streamed down my cheeks. Her gesture, and indeed its actual healing effects, would not have been possible if I hadn't first overcome my own sense of stigma about needing and seeking help, and then chipped away at it by being honest with other people about my mental health. Nearly a decade later, I'm still grateful to her. (Also, she was an amazing assistant and she's now an executive editor in her own right. Holla at Christine, everybody!)

When I moved on to my next job, I was doing much better anxiety-wise, so I didn't transport all of my talismans on to the next office. I poured out the sand and put the litter box in the recycling bin, but I took the beach painting and driftwood with me — more as decoration than medication, but, eh, tomato, tomahto. (Alas, the air plants turned out to be less indestructible than advertised.)

And by the time I left *that* job — which signaled the end of a whole career and way of life — I packed up some "essentials" from what would be my last corporate office and, apparently, tucked them away under the bed.

By the time I pulled out that box, I didn't really need my faux beach anymore. I'd already started building a house near a real one and was in the process of moving there permanently. I was calmer, healthier, and happier working for myself, and I'd been using the other techniques my doctor taught me (deep breathing, journaling, and a couple of prescription medications) — to manage my underlying anxiety and periodic bouts of panic.

But I hadn't thrown away the painting and the driftwood. And it's not because I hold on to gifts just for the sake of it. (Like a certain *other* guru, I believe a gift has fulfilled its destiny the minute it is gifted.) No, I think I kept them because they represented comfort and security. At that time, leaving them on the sidewalk would have felt like leaving my Xanax bottle in a taxi right before a transatlantic flight.

When I was eventually forced to make some decisions about what to put in a suitcase en route to the DR and what to leave on a Brooklyn street corner, I finally parted with my "beach." I had made significant strides to procure another one, after all, and I could use the room in my luggage to smuggle extra boxes of Imodium.

What? I'm all about candor, guys. Surely you know this by now.

**Owning the highs and lows of my mental health, talking about it openly, and getting professional help are what got me through a terrible, challenging time.**

They're what keep getting me through challenging

times, such as, for example, writing a third book in less than two years. Or when my soon-to-be-canonized husband starts a grease fire in the oven while I'm writing this chapter and I have to take to the streets in my bedhead and yoga pants to down-regulate. HOWDY, NEIGHBORS.

I've survived precisely *because* **I'm willing to "act crazy" in order to address my problems, head securely on and held high.** I'm willing to breathe deeply (four in through the nose, six out through the mouth) in a stalled elevator full of strangers. I'm willing to fill a prescription for Zoloft in broad daylight and also dig through my purse in front of someone I just met to find, uncap, and dry-swallow the pill I forgot to take this morning. I'm willing to keep a *motherfucking litter box under my desk in a corporate high-rise for a year* if it means warding off another panic attack.

Whatever works, bitches!

**So my advice to you is that it's okay to "act crazy" — and it might even be necessary.**

Yes, you may have to embarrass yourself a little in order to sidestep a lifetime of hidden shame and suffering. But if you're like me, once you try it and experience the benefits of brazen self-care, you won't actually be that embarrassed. You'll be too busy feeling relieved. And empowered. And maybe even happy. Again, I don't want to overstep my diagnostic or therapeutic bounds here, but I speak from experience.

My life got immeasurably better when I **stopped worrying about LOOKING like a crazy person and started ACTING like one.**

Maybe give it a shot? It's got to be better than a kick in the teeth.

# You Should Smile More*

## *How to break free from the Cult of Nice.

I'd like to begin this chapter with a shout-out to any readers who've been urged to "Smile!" while walking down the street minding their own goddamn business. Raise your hand if you know what it's like to unnaturally contort your face in order to avoid being singled out, criticized, or retaliated against.

This happened to me approximately EVERY DAY when I lived in New York City. No, I'm exaggerating. Every other day. On public transit, in a crosswalk, at a bodega — you name a locale and a stranger has told me that I should be smiling in it.

A passing cyclist once told me to smile as I stood outside my dentist's office postfillings, waiting for a cab; a cabdriver told me to smile after I narrowly escaped being assaulted at a stranger's apartment; and a guy on the subway told me to smile the day after I euthanized my cat.

What is it with these arbitrary demands on the formation of my lips, cheeks, and teeth? Who cares whether I look happy to be on my way to work or back from lunch or just having left the doctor's office after an invasive procedure? And why is it my responsibility to smile at all, especially *during the act of being harassed?*

SERIOUSLY WHAT IS THAT ABOUT CAN SOMEONE PLEASE EXPLAIN IT TO ME.

(It doesn't happen quite as much now that I live in the Dominican Republic, although a lot of people who definitely did not come out of my hoo-hah nevertheless address me as "Mami," accompanied by a distinct hissing/clicking noise that might mean "You should smile more" in a local dialect with which I am not yet familiar.)

Anyway, this whole chapter isn't about street harassment

### Reasons I might not be smiling on any given day

The next-door neighbors are playing "Despacito" on repeat.
A blister is forming on my pinky toe.
The US president is a sniveling, traitorous globule.
I'm about to have my period.
I'm having my period.
I just want to get out of here.

(though the daily struggle between resting bitch face and the patriarchy *is* real, it *is* an epidemic, and I'm happy to be the four millionth woman this week who's gone on record as saying so), but an unsolicited "Smile!" is emblematic of **a major obligation in the social contract: to LOOK or ACT or SAY SOMETHING nice when you have no desire or reason to do so.**

I'd like to talk about why that is total bullshit for everyone, not just the Resting Bitch Facers among us.

# The Cult of Nice

The Cult of Nice recruits across gender lines and doesn't distinguish between our personal and professional lives. It worships those who walk down the street grinning like they just watched America's *actual* funniest home video. It targets coworkers whose daily to-do lists include "expressing unwanted sympathy for your love life" and "making inane chitchat from the doorway while you're trying to get work done." And it elevates to godlike status those who are capable of biting their tongues when Uncle Pete brings up Hillary's emails at an otherwise pleasant family gathering. In 2028.

I mean no disrespect to card-carrying and aspiring cultists—it's impressive to be that nice all the time and I've got no beef with it. But what comes naturally to them might not come naturally to you or me, **and it is our prerogative to shut the door firmly in the face of would-be recruiters.**

> You want to walk around looking expressionless or morose? **Have at it.**

> You want to conserve time and energy by not engaging in small talk just to appear personable? **Fine by me.**

> You want to unleash the fury of a thousand Huma Abedins the next time Pete mumbles "Benghazi" through the pumpkin pie lodged in his jowls? **Make it so!** (Not only will I not stop you, if provided with enough advance notice I would happily show up and record this exchange for posterity.)

However, and as always, please don't take my acceptance of less-than-nice behavior as carte blanche to act all nasty.

I'm not trying to breed any American psychos here. I'm just saying that it's possible to be polite, productive, and professional without walking around sporting Howdy Doody's "O-face" on the regular.*

---

**Do as I do, not as I look when I'm walking down the street minding my own goddamn business**

One time when my husband and I were babies with virtually no disposable income, we splurged on a Valentine's Day dinner at a fancy restaurant. An older woman from his office was there, and she sent two glasses of champagne to our table just to be nice. She might as well have paid off our college loans, we were so delighted. As often as I can, I take a page out of that lady's handbook — because as much as forced, faux niceness makes me cringe, doing nice things for people for no other reason than because I really WANT to feels great! I wouldn't say it's right up there with heroin, but that's because I've never tried heroin. I *can* say, however, that doing nice things for people feels at least as good as chasing half a Valium with two airplane-sized bottles of Sutter Home Merlot.

---

* Come to think of it, that might actually be more terrifying than meeting Patrick Bateman in a dark alley.

Here are some tried-and-true methods for doing you without being supernice (or feeling superguilty) about it:

**When someone tells you that you'd look nice if you smiled more...**

...gaze directly into their eyes, unblinking, until they look away

...tell them you lost your cheek muscles in 'Nam

...wear a Bane mask on subsequent public outings

**When someone tells you that you could stand to "make nice" with family or coworkers...**

...say that "nice" is a relative term in that it does not apply to all your relatives

...tell them you would, but you're awfully busy getting shit done

...remind them that being nice didn't work out so well for a certain carpenter from Nazareth

**When someone tells you that if you don't have anything nice to say, you shouldn't say anything at all...**

...kindly refer them to the next section of this book.

# There's too much traffic on the high road

As a writer, I'm well acquainted with criticism, both valid and baseless. The valid stuff never feels good, but it comes with the territory and I accept it. The baseless stuff feels even less good, but you gotta laugh it off, ignore it, or not seek it out in the first place — especially if you are, according to Amelia from Amazon.com in a review of your first book, "a lying, selfish, arrogant, passive-aggressive monster, who has never faced real adversity in her entire life."

Would it be better if Amelia — who clearly had nothing nice to say — had decided not to say anything at all? Well, I don't *encourage* her brand of baseless criticism, but it's a free country (for now, at least) and she has every right.

What I *do* encourage is **not letting "nice" get in the way of defending yourself, your values, or the goddamn truth in the face of abject dickery**—assuming that you have valid provocation and engaging with the provocateur is worth it to you.

Way back in "How to be 'difficult,'" I talked about pushing for what you want and pushing back on what you don't. We covered collegial disagreements and differences of opinion on what constitutes the appropriate doneness of an eight-ounce filet. And I addressed peaceful cohabitation, better hotel rooms, and all of your boudoir needs, as well as having the courage of your convictions under the pressure to conform to someone else's point of view.

In each of these cases, my advice was heavy on **employing straightforward politeness to achieve your goals.** You don't have to leave menacing notes for your roommate or flip your boss's desk in order to make your feelings known.

And yet.

Occasionally you get provoked, and then there are only two ways forward:

1. You say nothing at all and someone else gets away with being an abject dick.

2. You decide to get NOT VERY NICE.

And I'm not talking garden-variety difficult, here, either. I'm talking a good old-fashioned, throat-clearing, deep-breath-taking, fixing-of-your-opponent-with-a-steely-gaze dressing down. Not just a clap back, a SLAP back (figuratively, of course).

If you find yourself in a position such as or akin to the following, I hope you'll feel comfortable saying something, even if it isn't nice:

**Situation:** Your Facebook friend announces that "climate change is a hoax."

**Response:** "Please note that, should you become trapped in rising floodwaters, your diseased brain cannot be used as a flotation device."

**Situation:** Your grandmother says, "If I'd known you'd put on so much weight, I would have bought you a bigger size."

**Response:** "It's a good thing that ugly sweatshirts, unlike family members, can be returned or exchanged!"

**Situation:** The plumber fails to show up within three hours of the appointed time...three times in a row.

**Response:** When he finally does fix the sink, use the memo section on your check to write "I HOPE YOU USE THIS MONEY TO BUY YOURSELF A WATCH, FUCKFACE."

When it comes to saying something nice, saying nothing at all, or getting all up in somebody's face, ask yourself two questions:

1. Is there valid provocation? (i.e., have you, your values, or the truth been assaulted?)

2. Is a not-nice response on your part worth (to you) any subsequent conflagration?

In the case of Me vs. Amelia from Amazon, yes to one, but "eh" to the second. I have better things to do. However, if the answer to both of those questions is a resounding "Hell yeah!" then you do you, my friend.

As a wise person* once said: "Two wrongs don't make a right — but it sure makes you feel good."

---

* My husband's friend Karen.

# You Shouldn't Eat That*

*I'll take extra cheese, please.*

For more than twenty years, I was on a diet. Sometimes it was a healthy one and sometimes an extreme version—and for at least five of those years, I was alternately anorexic and bulimic. In high school, in order to get and stay skinny I ran twenty-six miles every week, which may be the most un-me thing I've ever done besides winning a sports-based betting pool. (I did that once, but entirely by accident.)

My dieting history is far from unique. According to the National Eating Disorders Association (NEDA), "twenty million women and ten million men suffer from a clinically significant eating disorder sometime in their life." On their home page, NEDA states the obvious: The best-known contributor to the development of these illnesses is "body dissatisfaction," and they cite a 2011 study that says "By age six, girls especially start to express concerns about their own weight or shape. Forty to sixty percent of elementary school girls (ages six to twelve) are concerned about their weight or about becoming too fat. This concern endures through life."*

Well, slap my ass and call me jiggly. Who'd have thunk it? (I did. I thunk it. And chances are, you or someone you love has thunk it too.)

I was in a long-standing abusive relationship with my body, and those don't typically end well. But before I tell you how mine *did* end, let's take a look at how it started.

How did I get from being a kid with no awareness of whether my body was ideal or not, to an adolescent with acute "body dissatisfaction"? Apart from "general cultural bullshit," there were three comments that stand out in my mind:

> The first was a joke ("Your butt's eating your bathing suit!") that may have been intended solely to poke fun at my wedgie, or may have been an unsubtle hint that I was outgrowing said bathing suit. **I was nine or ten.**

—————

* www.nationaleatingdisorders.org

The second was a backhanded compliment delivered by a classmate who upon seeing me in — you guessed it — a bathing suit said quite sincerely, "Wow, you're not as fat as I thought you were." **I was eleven or twelve.**

The third came after I'd dropped forty pounds and three sizes. I'd just cut bangs into my long dark hair and someone said, "Doesn't she look like Karen Carpenter?" Another someone replied, "Yeah, BEFORE she got anorexic." What I heard was "before she got skinny." And since I had in fact become anorexic to lose all that weight but still wasn't, apparently, thin *enough* to look anorexic, I was confused. Was this a compliment? It didn't feel like one. **I was almost fourteen years old.**

In service to this chapter, I did some research to find out what Karen Carpenter weighed throughout her life. I learned that she was five feet, four inches tall (I'm 5' 2") and that before she started dieting around age sixteen, she weighed 145 pounds, which was about how much I weighed before I went on my first diet at thirteen. After she started dieting (initially, she claimed, to look better in her stage clothes), she got down to a reasonably healthy weight of 120 pounds and maintained that for several years before becoming severely ill and dipping into double digits on the scale.

When someone told me I looked like — again, to my ears — "fat," preanorexic, presumably 120-to-145-pound Karen Carpenter, I *weighed 99 pounds*.

Gee, no wonder I was confused.

Our society has a bad habit of valuing people based on their looks, and demeaning them when those looks don't match up with the "ideal." The ideal varies from culture to culture, but generally speaking, in order to be lauded for your figure you actually have to squirm your way into a demographic as tight and unforgiving as those leather pants Ross tried to pull off on the New Year's resolutions episode of *Friends*.

That's the worst part — when it comes to body shaming and the resulting body image issues, it's not like you're even trying to fit in where "most people" fall on the spectrum. **When it comes to our bodies, it isn't even good enough to be *average*.**

HOW. FUCKED. UP. IS. THAT.

Unfortunately, you cannot control the media's barrage of what constitutes the ideal form. You cannot inhabit the brains and mouths of those who offer thoughtless or cruel comments about your body that make you feel self-conscious or like you have to develop an eating disorder and run twenty-six miles in one week even though you hate running as much as the Dude hates the fucking Eagles, man.

Which is why I'm telling you: **You need to accept yourself before you wreck yourself.**

# It's all in your head, not in your hips

So how do you achieve acceptance, bodily or otherwise? Well, letting me blow sunshine up your back end is a start. I've been doing that since page 5. And remembering that we're all going to die — possibly tomorrow — is another useful technique. You could also just go on a diet, but this isn't a diet book, so I can't help you with that.

What I *can* help you with is learning how to tune out other people's criticism, your own neuroses, or both.

To be clear: I'm not claiming that some people don't need to lose (or gain) weight to address actual health problems rather than (or in addition to) confidence ones. I'm also not saying that people shouldn't be attuned to what they eat and concerned with how they look IF THAT BRINGS THEM JOY. Go ahead and do your Whole30 cleanse and your side planks if it makes you happy. You do you!

I just want you to know — if and only if you're interested — that **there's another way to get to self-acceptance that doesn't involve deprivation, carb counting, spin class, or shame.**

So...are you interested?

Okay, listen, you don't have to decide now. This chapter will be here for you in your time of need, should that time arise. But for the sake of argument, let's say that if body image is a problem for you, then one or more of the following is true:

- You ARE over- or underweight, by some metric. **Not a problem.**

- You have an ideal BMI but your mass is disproportionately located in places that make you self-conscious. Or maybe there's something else you don't like about your appearance — body image issues aren't confined to weight. **We can work with this, too.**

- You look absolutely "ideal" to even the most critical observer but you just don't see it when you look in the mirror. **You, my friend, are in for a treat.**

Buckle up, Buttercup, because this here's my hot take on all of the above:

- If you're over- or underweight, you can do your darnedest to lose or gain it, but society is still fucked and people are still assholes. Do you think you're going to reach the *Sports Illustrated* ideal (for men or women)? That seems…unlikely. Do you think assholes can't find another way to critique your appearance? Also unlikely.

- If you have a physical imperfection that you can't do much about — this coming from the woman who once said out loud to her boyfriend, "If I could have one plastic surgery with no pain or bad consequences I'd have my ankles thinned" — then you can't do much except accept it. (Or amputate.)

- And if you feel bad about your body for reasons neither you nor anyone else can understand, then it's not your body that's the problem, is it? It's all in your head, and THAT is my specialty.

One groovy solution to all of these problems is — you guessed it — mental redecorating. **Good old *fêng shui* with a side of "fuck that shit!"**

Mental redecorating can help *anyone* who feels bad about their body for *any* reason: too fat, too skinny, knees too knobby, boobs too big or too small, chest too narrow, thighs too spread-y, chin too prominent, whatever.

How? **Because it's not about changing your body, it's about changing your mind.**

And in the case of using mental redecorating to make peace with one's body, I'm like that guy in the Hair Club for Men commercials who exclaims, "I'm not just the president, I'm also a client!"

Here's how I did it:

- **Societal pressure is like faulty wiring in your house. You can't get rid of it entirely, but you can reroute and repair it.**

  I accepted that I would never have a physique that is "ideal" according to the culture I live in. My bones and muscles just aren't made that way. And I accepted that it wasn't worth my time or physical and emotional energy to beat myself up over two pounds or twenty, and that my value as a woman, a wife, a friend, a colleague, a beachgoer, or a human being was not tied up in the numbers on the scale or the letter on the tag on my bikini bottoms. My mental floor lamps still flicker occasionally when the connection gets overloaded, but overall, it's a big improvement.

- **Memories of mean shit people said about you are like unflattering photos you would never, ever frame and display.**

  I thought about all of the intentionally or unintentionally rude comments made about my body in the past, and I decided they didn't merit a place of honor on my mental shelves. I dumped them into a box in the back of my mental closet, and the only reason I dusted them off and brought them out in *You Do You* is to show you how it's done.

- **I learned how to take a fucking compliment every once in a while. Today, those compliments get matted, framed, and displayed in a place of honor where the ugly comments used to reside. And they sure do brighten up my mental living room.**

I *do* have a way with eye makeup — thanks for noticing!

This is how I slowly but surely redecorated my mental space — although I didn't call it "mental redecorating" then because I was not yet a fancy-pants anti-guru. I called it "a slowly dawning realization that if I didn't stop beating myself up about my size and shape, I might die of cardiac failure in my early thirties, and/or never experience a completely happy, carefree day in my whole motherfucking *life*."

You could also just call it **mind over matter**, because honestly, that's all it is.

It's what I've been saying through this whole book: **Do it yourself, because no one else can or will do it for you.** The same way nobody is going to do those sit-ups or suffer through that juice cleanse on your behalf, nobody but you has the power to get inside your head and instill you with confidence.

At my biggest, smallest, and sickest — even though I was lucky to have people around me telling me they loved me and I was beautiful — I never actually *felt* that way until I finally accepted myself for who I am, flaws and all.

**Acceptance breeds confidence.**

And confidence is what you really need — not just to rock those knobby knees or totally average thighs in a pair of short-shorts, but to be weird, make unconventional choices, fuck perfection, go your own way, and make the decisions that work best for YOU and YOUR life.

Like, for example, what kind of pizza to order tonight.

(No, seriously, guys, which one should I get? I've been fantasizing about it all day. Will it be my latest obsession, pepperoni and banana peppers? Or a white pie, thick with ricotta, drizzled in honey, and speckled with oregano? A classic New York–style "plain cheese" or a Margherita, topped with splotches of creamy fresh mozzarella and garnished with a handful of fresh basil leaves? Hmm . . . Probably not that last one. The basil sticks to the roof of my mouth—it's like trying to chew around a fragrant Band-Aid.)

But whichever one I choose, I can tell you this: I am going to enjoy the fuck out of it, I am not going to step on the scale tomorrow to see what pizza hath wrought, and I am not going to punish myself for days or weeks over a perfectly normal dinner that makes absolutely no difference to who I am or how I deserve to be treated— by myself or anyone else.

The world punishes us quite enough for eating and drinking and growing and shrinking, thank you very much. I'll save the self-flagellation for when I forget, yet again, to ask for crushed red pepper flakes on the side.

Dammit.

# You Should Check Your Ego at the Door*

### *Check to make sure it's fully inflated, that is.

After I got my first promotion to "big kid" status in my publishing career, I felt uncharacteristically unmoored. I'd had my old job for four years and could do it in my sleep, whereas the new gig came with a lot more autonomy and responsibility. I would finally have the chance to be difficult on my own behalf, and that was exciting, but also nerve-wracking.

What if I was a poser? What if my confidence in myself was misplaced? What if, it turned out, I couldn't cut it once I was called up from the minors to the Big Show?

That fall of 2005, I was twenty-six years old and trying to impress my new bosses, who had plucked a rather young editor to join the staff and gin up a new line of books. I was hiring an assistant for the first time (one not much younger than me), which made me feel sort of fraudulent, like *Who am I to command underlings?* And after only a few weeks, I'd already had a couple of run-ins with a new colleague who was, charitably speaking, a real piece of work.

In fact, I would say that out of the top five most infuriating things anyone has said to me in my life, this person was responsible for two of them — one of which forms the basis of this chapter, so THANKS, [NAME REDACTED]!*

## High fives all around

A month or so into my tenure, we editors had to do our first big formal presentation since I'd joined the company.

---

* If you and I ever find ourselves sidled up to the same watering hole, feel free to ask me about the other one. It's a gem.

I'd spent a lot of time writing and rehearsing my little spiels for each book I was responsible for. I knew I was blessed with a talent for good delivery (the Knight family has a motto, and that motto is "Perform or go to bed"), so of all the shit I was stressing about at that time, this had actually been relatively low on my list.

After the meeting — which had indeed gone well — I was in my office, exhaling and going over my notes. (Pertinent detail: My office was approximately the size of a U-Haul storage unit that Dexter might use to chop up some bodies, so whenever someone came and stood in my doorway I automatically felt trapped, and when [NAME REDACTED] appeared, my Spidey sense became extra-tingly.)

On this day, [NAME REDACTED] loomed over my petite threshold and casually asked how my pitch to the sales department had gone.

"Oh," I said, taken off guard by this display of mundane collegiality. "It was great, thanks! Public speaking is kind of my thing, though, so I wasn't too worried about it. How did yours go?"

At which point [NAME REDACTED] made a face as

though I had just declared time to be a flat circle, said, "Well, I wouldn't *congratulate* myself," then turned abruptly and stalked off down the hall.

*I wouldn't* congratulate *myself? What the fuck is that supposed to mean?*

Alone again in my office/storage unit, I spent the rest of the afternoon questioning whether I had been out of line, or too loudly tooted my own horn. Had I? Shit, it wasn't as though I'd leapt up from my swivel chair and shadowboxed around my office shouting "I'm not the greatest; I'm the double greatest! Not only do I knock 'em out, I pick the round!"

(Though in retrospect, that would have been awesome.)

In fact, the way I answered [NAME REDACTED]'s question had been calculated, or so I thought, to be *less* self-congratulatory. Just, you know, lucky me, I won the genetic lottery when it comes to shooting the shit for ten minutes in front of a small audience of book nerds. Nothing to see here, nothing to jump down my throat about, you mercurial shrew.

The more I thought about it, the more riled up I got. Because in reality, my successful performance *was* more than just luck. It took planning, preparation, skill, and yes, confidence. So if you're going to ask me how it went, why shouldn't I be candid about nailing it?

Why should anyone feel BAD about being confident?

# Leggo my ego

Like "selfish" and "negative," the word "ego" carries unfavorable connotations, and we both know that saying someone has a big one is never a compliment. It's always meant as an accusation of *over*confidence, whether or not that confidence is entirely justified.

So—and assuming that you are *not* the blustering, incompetent commander-in-chief of the world's most fearsome army, dangling your diminutive trigger finger over the nuclear codes—I'd like to use the final words of the final chapter of *You Do You* to disabuse you of the idea that having a small or medium-sized ego is a badge of honor.

It isn't.

**A healthy sense of self-esteem is not a flaw, and confidence is the greatest strength you can cultivate.** Your ego is where your confidence lies; ideally, it would be as capacious as an Olympic swimming pool and its contents as robust as the forearms on a Swedish lumberjack.

If someone doesn't like it, well, they are welcome to permanently park their opinion in the long-term lot located out behind their inferiority complex.

Unfortunately, and true to form, that place doesn't validate.

# That thorough stroking I promised

Well, champ, by now I hope you've internalized **the importance of self-acceptance** and picked up a few reliable strategies for achieving it. I hope you've seen the benefits of **acting with confidence** and learned how to muster it even under difficult circumstances.

And I hope you're ready to go out there and do you like Debbie did Dallas. You know what I mean.

But before we finish on the aforementioned zippy epilogue, I want to give you five more reasons to feel good about yourself and to pursue everything you want, need, and deserve out of life. Because you're good enough, you're smart enough, and doggone it, if people don't like or understand you — that's their problem, not yours.

---

**5 more reasons to feel good about yourself**

1. You don't back down when it seems like the world is out to get you. Instead, you seek to improve your situation. Well played, you.
2. You care about your friends and family — otherwise, you wouldn't have gone to the bookstore looking for ways to work around their bullshit.
3. You've got a lot to offer. I know this, because you offered your valuable time to get this far. And up to twenty-five units of your valuable currency, depending on which edition you bought.
4. You've [almost] finished a whole book. Congrats on being functionally literate or, in the case of audiobook listeners, knowing how to work an iPhone or a car stereo. The sky's the limit!
5. You're not dead yet.

---

# Epilogue

Things have been going pretty well lately, it's true, but there's still a vulnerable kid inside me who remembers what it was like to be picked on for the very qualities that would one day inform her biggest successes (in addition to being picked on for the dreaded Bionator, an orthodontic device that would cast a pall over her early teens).

That kid lives alongside a college student who exhausted and occasionally demeaned herself trying to make up for lost time, a young woman who felt uncomfortable being herself in the workplace, and a thirtysomething whose anxiety over making the "right" choices about how to look and act and work and live nearly broke her.

When I started writing this book, I was motivated by a desire to stick up for and help people like me who, at any time in their lives, have been made to feel that there is something wrong with them when there really isn't.

If you operate outside social norms, I wanted to support you, rather than giving you a book—like so many others on the self-help shelves—that urges you to conform to them. (*How to Get Rich! How to Be Skinny! How to Act Sane!*) I wanted to show that you don't have to change who you are—physically, intellectually, sartorially, whatever—in order to accept and thrive on being yourself. And I wanted to rally all of us against the Judgy McJudgersons who can't see past their own hang-ups to treat others with respect.

But *as* I was writing this book, I realized something that's changed the way I look at myself and the world—possibly more than any of the unconventional wisdom I've shared with you so far.

**I realized that we are all Judgy McJudgerson.**

Even me.

Like, I still don't understand how anyone can let their surfaces gather grime and their corners teem with cobwebs. When I see that kind of thing, I want to pull out my hair (or start pulling dust cloths from my sleeves like my alter ego, an excessively tidy clown named Mister Swiffers).

I also don't understand how anyone can talk about their toddler's Kung Fu class for twenty minutes with a straight face, and it seems I have heretofore been incapable of not interjecting my own snarky commentary into such a monologue.

And I *really* don't understand why a human being would be willing to share their bed with a dog. This is officially beyond my capacity for comprehension. Dogs. Eat. Their. Own. Poop.

Apparently, as accepting as I thought I was about people doing whatever works to get themselves through the day, I still harbor prejudices and make judgments about those who do things differently from me. And I often can't help but express it. It's like a compulsion.

So in order to practice what I preach, over the last few months I've doubled down on my efforts to be nonjudgmental — or at least to not actually say something (or whip out my portable DustBuster) when I can't help mentally critiquing someone's choices. And I have learned that it's REALLY HARD not to let microjudgments tiptoe off my tongue. I catch myself all the time now — either right before or, more regrettably, *while* I'm saying something critical.

Before my little epiphany, I always thought I was helping when I pointed out (even in jest, which is often how I point things out) that the way a person was living their life was inconsistent with my own *clearly correct* and *much better* way of doing things. I was only trying to guide them down a better path...wasn't I?

Right. Where have I heard that before? Oh yes, on page 209 of my own goddamn book:

> Clearly she thought she was helping — the same way everyone who tells me I'll regret not having children thinks they're doing me a favor, saving me from myself. But most of us don't need saving. We just need permission to be ourselves.

Well, well, well. It appears that what started out as a defiant manifesto about **accepting who you are and acting with confidence** has turned into something that even its author wasn't anticipating. *You Do You* **also means accepting other people for who *they* are, and acting with deference.**

That's a pretty neat trick, if the author does say so herself.

And get this: Paying more attention to not making someone else feel "less than" has made me a calmer, happier person. Thinking twice about passing judgment on others has lightened a burden of innate antagonism I didn't realize I was carrying. (Also a neat trick.) And declining to engage with that noise in my head has reduced unnecessary friction between me and people I love and respect.

I think that's officially a hat trick.

Yet — and in keeping with the preceding three hundred pages of promise and instruction — I haven't changed who I AM. It's not like I've forced myself to accept dust in my coffee mugs and dog hair on my pillow as a way of life. *My* life, I mean. I'm just trying to change the way I respond to those expressions of other people's perfectly normal, perfectly legitimate selves.

Which, when I think about it, disproves another frequent claim in this book — that I can't change the Judgy McJudgersons among us. Apparently, I can! Perhaps you'll be so kind as to leave a copy on your favorite Judgy's doorstep when you're finished?

What I'm saying, cats and kittens, is that at the end of the day we all have our shit. We all have our hang-ups, everybody's different, and then everybody dies. But in the meantime, life could be a whole lot better if you start looking out for number one — and stop getting your panties in a bunch over whatever numbers two, three, and four are up to.

You do you, and you'll do just fine.

Oh, and remember...

# IF YOU'RE

# NOT

# DOING YOU,

# YOU'RE

# SCREWING

# YOU.

# Acknowledgments

*You Do You* may be a tribute to self-reliance and individuality, but it would not exist without the hard work, help, and thorough strokings of my ego provided by the following people:

Jennifer Joel is always looking out for my best interests (as though I don't do enough of that already), and there is nobody I would rather have in my corner. She makes being "difficult" look easy, not to mention likable and stylish. She's not just my agent, she's my hero.

Michael Szczerban has been letting me do me for three books now, but his spot-on notes, insightful queries, and a few of his own chortle-worthy jokes have made each of them better than I ever hoped they could be. He is the gentlest of dumplings.

His colleagues at Little, Brown — including but not limited to Ben Allen, Reagan Arthur, Ira Boudah, Amanda Brown, Sabrina Callahan, Nicky Guerreiro, Lauren Harms, Andy LeCount, Nel Malikova, Katharine Meyers, Lauren Passell, Barbara Perris, Lauren Velasquez, and Craig Young — are keeping the no-fucks-given flame alive. Thanks, guys! If I have to play on a team, I'm glad it's with you.

Natasha Hodgson at Quercus Books was the very first to express her enthusiasm for *You Do You,* and I'm grateful to her and her colleagues — Bethan Ferguson, Charlotte Fry, Elizabeth Masters, and Laura McKerrell — for their gloriously inventive support of my books and me over the years. Jane Sturrock, now back and with 100 percent more Sophie, rounds out a substantial cheering section.

Additional thanks to all-stars Sharon Green, Lindsay Samakow, and Nic Vivas at ICM; Lisa Cahn from Hachette Audio; Callum Plews, Gavin Skal, and Audiomedia Production; and to the readers all over the world who clamored for one more. (Big ups to Poland, by the way. You guys give mad Instagram love.)

To my parents: Thank you for instilling in me good values and a strong moral compass, despite what Amelia from Amazon might think. And thank you for not smothering me with my blanket. I remember the time I wouldn't stop screaming until Dad drove halfway back to Camden to retrieve it for me, and that night alone must have been extremely tempting.

Finally, the biggest slice of my large cheese pizza of gratitude goes to my husband, Judd Harris, who makes sure I'm always well-fed, well-slept, and well-spritzed. He is a profoundly weird contrarian nonconformist, and that is exactly why I love him.

# About the Author

 Sarah Knight's first book, *The Life-Changing Magic of Not Giving a Fuck,* has been published in eighteen languages and counting, and her TEDx talk, "The Magic of Not Giving a Fuck," has more than two million views. The second book in the No Fucks Given guides series, *Get Your Shit Together,* is a *New York Times* bestseller. Her writing has also appeared in *Glamour, Harper's Bazaar, Marie Claire, Red, Refinery29,* and elsewhere. After quitting her corporate job in 2015 to pursue a free-lance life, she moved from Brooklyn, New York, to the Dominican Republic, where she currently resides with her husband and a shitload of lizards.

You can learn more at sarahknightauthor.com, follow her on Twitter and Instagram @MCSnugz, or sign up for her No Fucks Given newsletter at tinyletter.com/sarahknight.

# Also available

**The Life-Changing Magic of Not Giving a F**k**

The no-f**ks-given international bestseller

How to stop spending time you don't have doing things you don't want to do with people you don't like

Sarah Knight

'Genius'
*Cosmopolitan*

'Works a charm'
*Sunday Times Magazine*

'Life-affirming'
*Guardian*

**Get Your Sh*t Together**

Bestselling author of *The Life-Changing Magic of Not Giving a F**k*

How to stop worrying about what you should do so you can finish what you need to do and start doing what you want to do

Sarah Knight

'Genius'
*Vogue*

'I love Knight'
*Sunday Times Magazine*

'The anti-guru'
*Observer*

# Praise for Sarah Knight

"Genius" — *Cosmopolitan*

"Life-affirming" — *Guardian*

"Absolutely blinding. Read it. Do it" — *Daily Mail*